If You Voted for Obama in 2008 to Prove You're Not a Racist, You Need to Vote for Someone Else in 2012 to Prove You're Not an Idiot

by

Neil Snyder

Contents

About the Author

Neil Snyder taught strategy and leadership at the University of Virginia for 25 years before retiring in 2004 and moving to Lake Hartwell in South Carolina. He is the author of numerous books including *Vision, Values & Courage*, *The Will to Lead*, *His Name is Yahweh*, *Stand!*, *Falsely Accused*, and *What Will You Do with the Rest of Your Life?* He has published more than 100 articles and business case studies. Currently, he is the Ralph A. Beeton Professor of Free Enterprise Emeritus at the University of Virginia.

During his tenure at UVA, Dr. Snyder served as Policy Advisor for Regulatory Reform to Governor Charles S. Robb of Virginia (1982-1985); he was co-chairman in 1985 and chairman in 1986 of the Governor's Conference on Small Business in Virginia; and in 1985, he received the Small Business Advocacy Award of the Virginia Chamber of Commerce. He has worked with GE, the Federal Bureau of Investigation, the Drug Enforcement Administration, and the Department of Defense, among others.

Chapter 1

The 2012 Presidential Election will be Won or Lost in the Middle

First things first. I didn't come up with the title for this book. A friend sent me an email that included a picture of a sign that a man posted in his front yard. In bold letters, the sign read, "If you voted for Obama in 2008 to prove you're not a racist, you need to vote for someone else in 2012 to prove you're not an idiot." I liked it because it was appropriate and catchy, so I decided to use it as the title for this book.

I know people personally who voted for Obama in 2008 because he's a black man, and they wanted the people of the United States to elect a black president. They were half right. Barack Obama is half black and half white, but that nuance didn't matter to them. His lack of experience didn't matter either. Neither did his nefarious connections or his Chicago-style thug politics. Nothing mattered to them except electing a black man even if he was only half black.

Rationalizing his decision to vote for Obama, one friend told me that presidents can't do too much damage. He was wrong, and I cautioned him that presidents can do a lot of harm to this country and to our allies. Three years later, after the damage has been done already, he agrees with me. He won't make the same mistake again, or so he says, but defeating a sitting president at the polls won't be easy.

Until the day he leaves office, President Obama will have the power of the purse, and he has proven that he does one thing well. He can give away our hard-earned money to people who support him with the best of them. He makes Richard Nixon look like a choirboy in that respect. He'll use our money to buy as many votes as he can, and he'll do it legally because he is the President of the United States thanks to some of my friends and like-minded people who voted with their hearts instead of their heads in 2008.

Obama will also have the bully pulpit as long as he is president, but he has abused that advantage. His gift of gab is turning against him. Most Americans don't bother to watch or listen to him any longer since they've heard it all before—many times. The president must not realize that people are tuning him out. He continues to seek airtime during primetime to make the same worn-out speeches, and the words, the cadence, and the finger pointing are the same from speech-to-speech. Even the pregnant pauses for applause are the same—only the adoration he covets is getting harder to come by.

That's history. We have to turn our attention to the 2012 election. The most effective way to approach this campaign is to get familiar with the facts and tell everyone we know about them. This book is about what Barack Obama has actually done as president. It's not a political diatribe, and it's not based on opinions. It simply lays out the facts for thinking people to consider. That should be enough for most Americans. They may not take the time to search out the facts, but they will think about them if someone they know and trust presents them in an articulate way or if they read a book like this one. Some of them, hopefully most of them, will want to know more, and they will do a little digging. If they do, they will be convinced because the facts are compelling arguments for not re-electing Barack Obama.

I realize that dyed-in-the-wool Obama supporters, the Obamanistas as I call them, will be offended by this statement, but no thinking person who understands the facts will cast a vote for Barack Obama. That means the president will have to depend on his diehard cadre of Obamanistas to win re-election, and their numbers are dwindling rapidly because as president Barack Obama has managed to do nothing right. That does not mean that he won't be a formidable candidate, because at the end of the day, he is still a black man, or half black, and he is the President of the United States.

You Will be Called a Racist if You Oppose Barack Obama

I need to give you a warning before you read any further. Anyone who opposes Barack Obama will be called a racist. Obamanistas believe name-calling is the secret weapon that will bring them victory in 2012. I can't fault them too much because that's the only arrow in their quiver that has a sharp point. All the others have dull tips or no points at all because they've been blunted by the president's performance. That's why Obamanistas can't use the facts and can't defend him against the facts, so get ready. They will call you a racist or anti-science or backward or a Neanderthal or worse. Unfortunately, that strategy will work on some people since no one wants to be vilified. Don't give in to their abuse. Stand your ground and tell people what you know.

One more thing. I was a Democrat from the time I was a child until 1986. That's when I completed my assignment as Governor Chuck Robb's (D-Virginia) Policy Advisor for Regulatory Reform. When I understood what the Democratic Party stands for, I had no choice but to get out. The Democratic Party today stands for 3 things:

1. the "right" of a woman to take the life of her unborn child for any reason whatsoever without fear of consequence,

2. the "rights" of perverted people to practice their perversions openly without penalty or even criticism, and

3. the creation of a socialist welfare state where the federal government is in charge of almost everything.

That's why Obamanistas will never relent. President Obama is their man even though he has a miserable performance record because he stands for what they believe in most. Don't waste your time trying to persuade an Obamanista to switch sides. You would be more successful trying to convince a skunk not to stink.

Obama's Gift of Gab is a Double-edged Sword

President Obama loves to talk. His penchant for giving speeches is based on his demonstrated success on the stump and his belief that "talking" and "doing" are synonymous. Talking is one of Obama's problems too—probably his most significant problem. He talks too much. Even his most enthusiastic supporters know that.

Several catchphrases find their way into most of Obama's speeches. For example,

- "This is not about me."
- "I inherited the worst economy since the Great Depression."
- "Let me be perfectly clear."
- "George Bush…(fill in the blank)."

After a great deal of criticism, the president finally stopped referring to George Bush by name so conspicuously in connection with his economic woes, but he still points his finger at Bush whenever his performance is called into question. Obama also continues to pepper his speeches with his now famous lines "this is not about me" and "let me be perfectly clear," but everything he does and says is about him. That much is perfectly clear.

Barack Obama's gift of gab is a double-edged sword. One side of the blade wins him adoration and support. The other side of the blade infuriates his political opposition. Thankfully, Obama is not a great communicator on a par with Ronald Reagan, for example. He hasn't mastered the art of softening blows that invigorate the right side of the political spectrum. That's why you don't see Republicans leaving the fold and crossing over to join Obama the way a significant number of Democrats did when Reagan ran against Jimmy Carter in 1980.

Obama's tendency to talk first and think later is a tremendous weakness that we can and should exploit. His off-the-cuff remarks reveal his true character and embolden those who see what he's trying to accomplish. People in the middle of the political spectrum aren't paying close attention. They seldom do. That's why Obama won the election in 2008. People in the middle have to be reminded often about what is taking place right in front of them and about how high the stakes are in 2012.

We have another advantage in 2012—something that we didn't have in 2008. President Obama has a performance record this time around, and it's not good. Even so, the vast majority of voters can be persuaded to believe almost anything, and they will believe almost anything unless we do our job and tell them the facts.

The 2012 Presidential Election will be Won or Lost in the Middle

Thankfully, Obamanistas are not in the majority. They reside on the far left of the political spectrum—so far left, in fact, that they try to hide their true identities. They know that the general public would never accept their ideas if they presented them all at once, so they dole them out piecemeal.

One by one, little by little they introduce parts of their plan, and people hardly notice that things are changing. They go along willingly because they don't see the master plan. It's like the story about the bullfrog. As the story goes, if you toss a bullfrog into boiling water, he will jump out and save himself because he has strong legs and quick reflexes, but if you place him in cold water and heat it up slowly, he will eventually die because he doesn't realize that the water is getting hotter.

That's the approach preferred by the far left because it works. We adjust to the world they're fashioning slowly and methodically in front of our eyes, and we do it without making much of a fuss since the individual changes although offensive to some seem minor to most. While the far left holds the reins of power, the White House in particular, they use tax dollars to buy off vocal critics, and the general public barely notices that a battle is raging.

Barack Obama is a far left person. He's probably the most far left president the United States has ever had. People with his political beliefs are unelectable in a general election—that is, of course, unless they can convince voters that they aren't who they appear to be. Obama's oratory skills will win over people in the middle of the political spectrum who are uninformed and unwilling to expend the effort to get the facts. That's where we come in. Our job is to give them the facts—neatly packaged and easy to understand.

After three years on the job, President Obama can't run in 2012 on abstract promises about hope and change unless we let him. His performance record is a millstone around his neck, but it will mean nothing if we don't do our job.

The 2012 presidential election will be won or lost in the middle. People in the middle can be persuaded by facts. That's what we have to deliver to them and that's what this book is all about. It lays out facts for thinking people to consider.

John Adams said, "Facts are stubborn things," and the facts tell a story about President Obama that will keep him from winning a second term in office. But the facts have to be communicated. That's why you need to read this book and share it.

President Obama said, "I just have to remind people that here's one thing I know for certain: The odds of me being reelected are much higher than the odds of me being elected in the first place."[1]

He's right. Even though the facts are against him, the odds of Obama being re-elected are much higher than the odds of him being elected in 2008, and you know what happened in 2008. Don't take anything for granted. President Obama owns the bully pulpit and he controls the purse strings. This battle won't be easy, but working together, we can make a difference, so let's get started.

---

[1] http://campaign2012.washingtonexaminer.com/blogs/beltway-confidential/obama-odds-are-ill-get-re-elected

Chapter 2

Barack Obama is an Economic Disaster

It's an undeniable fact that the economic problems President Obama inherited when he took office were created by presidents who preceded him. That's the way things work in our country and it's the nature of our political system, but the problems confronting Obama in 2009 when he became president were spawned in 1977[2] when Congress passed The Community Reinvestment Act[3] (CRA). Jimmy Carter was president at the time, and the CRA survived through Presidents Ronald Reagan, George Bush the father, Bill Clinton, and George Bush the son.

Bill Clinton did more than any other president to impose sloppy lending practices on the banking community, but George W. Bush gets most of the blame even though he actually tried to do something about it. His efforts met tremendous resistance in Congress, and he didn't push the issue the way he should have. President Bush deserves criticism for not doing enough to deal with the housing bubble before it exploded, but President Clinton should get the lion's share of the blame along with his liberal progressive comrades in Congress—people like Representative Barney Frank (D-Massachusetts) and Senator Chris Dodd (D-Connecticut).

That said, the 2012 presidential campaign is not about George W. Bush because he is not on the ballot. It's not about Jimmy Carter, Ronald Reagan, George Bush the father, or Bill Clinton either. The 2012 presidential election will be a referendum on Barack Obama's performance, so you can rest assured that Obamanistas will do

---

[2] http://www.policylink.org/site/c.lkIXLbMNJrE/b.5136939/k.8577/Community_Reinvestment_Act.htm

[3] http://www.federalreserve.gov/communitydev/cra_about.htm

everything they can to divert attention away from Obama's performance and toward anything that will silence his critics. Our job is to make sure they don't get away with it.

Can our economy be fixed?

I'm a regular guest on a weekly radio talk show on WJJC in Commerce, Georgia—a town just outside the Atlanta area—titled "America in Crisis." I grew up in Athens, Georgia with one of the show's co-hosts, John Gaissert, and I've gotten to know the other co-host, Craig Fischer, over the air. One day John asked me if we could save our economic system, and I said "yes, but..."

Yes our economic system can be saved. In fact, saving it isn't difficult from a theoretical perspective, but in the real world saving it will be very difficult. Here's why:

- The United States is the world's richest nation in terms of energy resources, but we're not developing the abundant resources we have. We possess enough coal, oil, and natural gas to meet our energy needs for hundreds of years and to export our surplus energy thus tapping into an enormous tax revenue stream. Why aren't we doing it? Answer: it's because of people like Barack Obama.

- We are borrowing vast sums of money to stimulate the economy at a time when our debt/GDP ratio is approaching 100% thus making the dollar a suspect currency at best. Since we already have about $15 trillion in debt, that's not a harbinger of great things to come, but we give scant attention to the stimulative effects of tax cuts on job creation and economic growth. We are in the process of turning the United States into a socialist country at a time when capitalism is surging around the world—even in places like China. What's the problem? Answer: people like Barack Obama.

- Approximately 50% of our fellow citizens pay no federal income taxes and more than 40% of our fellow citizens take more money out of our system than they put in. If that's not evidence of a socialist system in the making, I don't know what is. Why are we moving down a path that has failed in every country where it's been tried? Answer: people like Barack Obama.

- Healthcare spending in the United States is just under 18% of our GDP, and healthcare costs are spiraling out of control. Healthcare costs alone can bankrupt this nation, and Medicare just keeps footing the rising bill for our seniors despite evidence that we can't continue down this path without destroying our country. We need reform, serious reform, but we're not getting it. Why? Answer: it's because of people like Barack Obama.

Rather than helping to solve our nation's problems, President Obama has made them worse by doing everything in his power to stifle energy production, by showing callous disregard for our debt and deficit problems, and by shoving his socialist agenda down our throats against our will. Obamacare is a perfect example of this, but it is by no means the only example.

We need a problem solver as president, and Barack Obama is not that person. President Obama instinctively runs from problems until he can't avoid them any longer, and then he tries to place the blame for our problems on others. That's not leadership, and that approach won't get us out of the mess we're in.

Budget Details that You Need to Know

A recent article in *American Thinker* by Greg Richards titled "Where the Budget Deficit Actually Came From"[4] presents important information about our fiscal crisis and shows why we have a huge and growing debt problem. For instance,

1. There is no "Social Security Trust Fund." The SSTF is nothing more than IOUs from the federal government because SS surpluses have been used to pay for ongoing government operations and to hide our huge and growing deficit problem for years. Even President Clinton's so-called "budget surpluses" were just a mirage. If unfunded SS liabilities had been factored in properly, there would have been no surpluses. The SS surplus began a steep decline in 2008. It will continue to fall and eventually will be eliminated completely as more and more Baby Boomers retire. Simply stated, the day of SSTF chicanery is over, and it's time to deal with the problem.

2. Medicare spending is a huge problem. It's growing like Topsy, and there is no end in sight. Left unchecked, rapidly increasing SS and Medicare costs will bankrupt this nation. When you add interest on the debt, the problem only gets worse.

3. At current levels, unemployment security spending in the United States is roughly 75% of defense spending. Stated another way, we are paying almost as much to keep people unemployed as we are to defend our country.

I'll stop there, but I think a little explanation about point number 3 is in order. I'm not a coldhearted person, and I understand the need for unemployment benefits.

---

[4] http://www.americanthinker.com/2011/04/where_the_budget_deficit_actua_1.html

That said, we have turned unemployment into a career for a large and growing number of people in our country. For them, unemployment is little more than another welfare payment, and since the government continues to extend unemployment benefits, some of our fellow citizens feel no pressing need to find a job.

I liken this problem to the generational welfare problem we heard so much about in the 1990s. If we don't come to grips with it now, we will create a permanent underclass in the United States made up of the chronically unemployed. That is far more callous than letting unemployment benefits expire after a reasonable amount of time. The underemployment issue is important as well. It will remain a problem until our economy improves and begins creating jobs again.

Plato said, "Necessity is the mother of invention." He was right. There is no better way to focus the mind than to remove artificial support. President Obama has done nothing during his term as president to help solve these problems. His signature piece of legislation, Obamacare, is anything but a solution. In fact, it makes our problems worse because it imposes the cost of socialized medicine on the federal government—costs the federal government can ill afford to pay. Alternatives to Obamacare that might have worked were never given any consideration by President Obama and his loyalists in the House and Senate led by Nancy Pelosi and Harry Reid. You can bet that President Obama condoned and/or motivated their intransigence.

President Obama has avoided our Social Security problem like the plague. When he's been forced to address it, he has done little more than demagogue the issue to win favor in the minds of senior citizens. That isn't leadership and it won't solve our problem, but you can be certain about this fact. Our deficit and debt problems will continue to grow until we get a grip on Social Security, Medicare, and Medicaid spending. In fact, entitlement spending in general needs to be thought through from top to bottom. President Obama's lack of performance in these critical areas is a good reason not to re-elect him.

We Have Created an Unsustainable Welfare State

We are approaching a tipping point in the United States where the majority of our citizens will contribute nothing toward national defense, education, and the myriad social programs that have been set up to support people who pay no taxes. In fact, we may have reached the tipping point already.

The numbers are frightening. In 2008,

- the top 1% of earners in the United States paid 38% of federal income taxes;

- the top 5% of earners paid 59% of federal income taxes;

- the top 10% of earners paid 70% of federal income taxes;

- the top 25% of earners paid more than 86% of federal income taxes;

- the top 50% of earners paid more than 97% of federal income taxes;

- and the bottom 50% of earners in the United States paid less than 3% of federal income taxes.

In 2009, the top 10 percent of earners in the United States paid about 73 percent of federal income taxes, and about 47 percent of our fellow citizens paid no federal income taxes. In 2009, the bottom 40 percent of earners actually made a profit on tax day because they got more money back from the federal government than they paid in.

When people who pay no taxes and receive the lion's share of the benefits represent the majority, you can expect them to vote in their own self-interest, and what will that be? They will vote for candidates like Barack Obama who promise to continue funding programs that funnel money to them and to tax the rich to pay for the programs. In the process, they will destroy this nation. Our nation's deficit and debt problems make it perfectly clear that their influence is being felt already, and as I said, we may have reached the point of no return. If Barack Obama is re-elected, the end of the United States as we know it may be in sight. That's why I believe the 2012 presidential election is the most important election in our nation's history. We have our work cut out for us. If we don't change course now, we may seal our nation's fate.

As Democratic politicians pump up their rhetoric about "fairness" and play the class warfare game to curry favor with voters, keep these things in mind. Our current trajectory leads to insolvency. We engage in wild-eyed deficit spending and pretend that there are no consequences; we have piled up almost $15 trillion of debt; and we are forecasting huge deficits as far as the eye can see. This can't continue. Our creditors will make sure that they don't if we fail to take action ourselves.

A friend and regular SnyderTalk (www.snydertalk.com) reader sent me an email after reading one of my editorials. In the editorial, I focused on the inherent danger we face as a nation because very soon a majority of our fellow citizens will pay no federal income taxes at all. My friend who is a Democrat, an Obama supporter, and a businessman from Texas told me that I need to broaden my focus and zero in on things like

- subsidies to farmers,

- bank bailouts,

- military subcontractors who overcharge taxpayers by billions of dollars,

- cattle rancher subsidies,

- oil subsidies, and

- lack of fair tariffs on goods brought into this country by corporations that have their products made overseas.

He's right. We need a complete overhaul. We need tax reform and spending reform from top to bottom. We can't continue to spend money we don't have on things we don't need, and we can't tax the rich into oblivion while we transfer their wealth to the poor. I use the word "poor" with great hesitation since 50% of our fellow citizens are NOT POOR. Most of them are simply freeloading. I think that's the most important danger we face since the welfare mindset and the freeloader mindset are passed on to children, and we create a generational problem with which we must contend. Truth is we've already done it.

My friend also said, "If you leave it up to politicians of both parties, it (significant change) will never happen." He's right again. There is plenty of blame to go around. Both Republicans and Democrats created the mess we're in, and trusting career politicians to fix the system is like trusting the fox to guard the henhouse. To say the least, it's fraught with risk.

Barack Obama is a perfect example of a career politician. He has never done anything substantive in his life except hold public office, and those who voted for him for president looking for hope and change got neither. His administration is worse than the same old same old. He's trying to remake our free enterprise system into a socialist system that's destined to fail. I say "destined to fail" since socialism has failed everyplace it's been tried.

There will be kicking and screaming when we reform our system, but we can't maintain the status quo and survive as a nation. Barack Obama has done nothing to help solve our problems. In fact, he has made them worse. His liberal progressive socialist agenda and his demagoguery may work in Chicago, but it doesn't work in the rest of the country and it won't solve our problems.

If you weren't worried about our deficit and debt problems before Monday April 18, 2011, you had better start worrying now.

Monday April 18, 2011—a date which will live in infamy. That's the day that the credit rating firm Standard & Poor's lowered the long-term outlook for United States debt to negative. Their criteria indicated that there was a 1-in-3 chance that by 2013 they would downgrade United States Treasury bonds from the AAA level. That's important because lower ratings translate into higher interest rates on our almost $15 trillion and growing national debt.

Following a charade in Congress posing as a debt ceiling debate, Standard & Poor's did downgrade United States bonds to the AA+ level. Obviously, our political leaders weren't paying attention or they just didn't care. President Obama did virtually nothing to prevent the downgrade from happening except to criticize Standard & Poor's. The problem isn't Standard & Poor's. The problem is Barack Obama and other liberal progressive politicians who either don't understand our economy or don't care about the effects of their decision. Whatever the case may be, they have taken this country to the precipice, and it's our job to win it back.

Liberal progressive Svengalis tell us that we don't actually owe $15 trillion since almost $5 trillion of our debt is money owed to the Social Security Trust Fund. I'm sure that nugget of wisdom will enable our seniors to sleep well at night. They can rest soundly knowing that their Social Security deductions all those years were used to pay for everything under the sun, and now the money they need in retirement is tied up in IOUs from the federal government. What could be safer? According to Standard & Poor's, they would be better off owning French debt.

It wasn't a coincidence that Standard & Poor's chose to sound the alarm on Tax Day 2011 just in time for the debate about raising the debt ceiling, and it wasn't by chance that they cut our bond rating immediately following the so-called "debate."

They must have been as enthusiastic as I was about the "historic" $38.5 billion in spending cuts that were announced as part of the Great Budget Compromise. As it turns out, instead of cutting spending by $38.5 billion in 2011 as we were told by President Obama, House Speaker Boehner, and Majority Leader Reid, the actual spending reduction amounted to only about $352 million in 2011. That's less than a rounding error given the fact that federal spending for 2011 was just under $4 trillion.

I'm encouraged that the people at Standard & Poor's recognize budget chicanery when they see it. I just hope the American people do, and it's our job to educate them.

The United States doesn't have a revenue problem. With the exception of the Great Recession and the 2001-2002 recession, the revenue side of our income statement has shown healthy growth. Our problem is spending. It's been completely out of control for more than a decade, and the Great Recession only made our spending problem worse—much worse. At this point, our debt load has reached an alarming level, and I mean that literally. As they say, it's time to pay the fiddler.

The charts on the next page show federal spending per household and total federal revenue. Examining them should convince you that we have a spending problem—not a revenue problem. Revenue growth has been impressive, but spending growth has outstripped revenue growth by a wide margin. Notice that spending growth started accelerating rapidly while George Bush was president, and it took off like a rocket when Barack Obama became president.

To put our debt problem in perspective, consider this fact. In 2010 according to the International Monetary Fund,[5] the United States debt/GDP ratio was 92.7%. That's a problem because Standard & Poor's starts to worry about a country's ability to manage

---

[5] http://en.wikipedia.org/wiki/List_of_sovereign_states_by_public_debt

its finances when its debt/GDP ratio reaches 80%. Unless things change, in the not too distant future, we won't be able to see 80% in the rearview mirror.

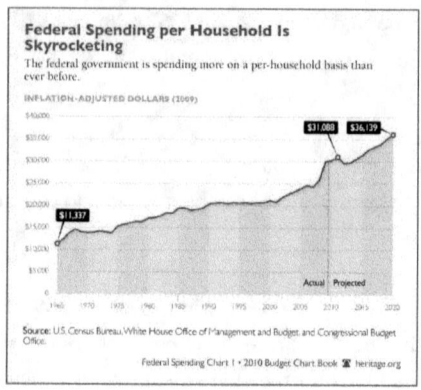

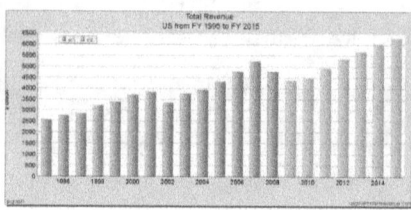

The chart on the next page shows the United States debt/GDP ratio from 1900 to today. It shows that Presidents Bush and Obama have contributed greatly to our nation's debt problems, but Bush is no longer president. Obama is, and he doesn't get it. Even worse, he doesn't seem to care.

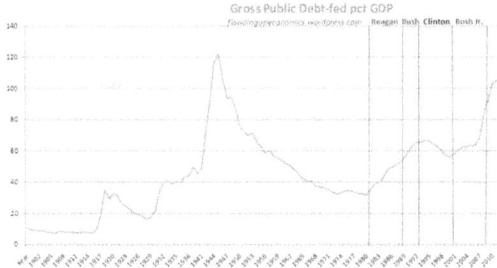

Gross Public Debt-fed pct GDP

How does the United States' debt/GDP ratio compare[6] with the debt/GDP ratios of up-and-coming economic powerhouse nations? Take a look:

- Brazil's debt/GDP ratio for 2010 is 66.8%;

- Russia's debt/GDP ratio for 2010 is 11.1%;

- India's debt/GDP ratio for 2010 is 71.8%; and

- China's debt/GDP ratio for 2010 is 19.1%.

I'm always amused when liberal progressive pundits and politicians tell us that the solution to our deficit and debt problems is to raise taxes on the rich. The data I've presented already shows how ridiculous that argument is. Even so, feeling the pressure because of criticism Obama has received for continually suggesting that "the rich" must pay more, White House spokesman Jay Carney told the press that people who don't pay federal income taxes do pay payroll taxes. In other words, they aren't getting off scot-free. That's the quality of analysis I've come to expect from the Obama team. Every wage earner in America pays payroll taxes, including the rich if they have jobs. As I said, the chicanery never ceases, and the Obama White House is good at obfuscation.

---

[6] http://en.wikipedia.org/wiki/List_of_sovereign_states_by_public_debt

This is the bottom line. It's time for us to get serious about our deficit and debt problems because we don't have much time left. Either we will get our act together, or our creditors will tell us what we have to do. Ironically, that's what we used to do. We were the ones telling other countries that they couldn't keep borrowing and spending. We were brutal as we forced nations to implement austerity measures so they could remain solvent. Now the tables are turning, and they're telling us. Problem is Barack Obama isn't listening or he has a hearing impairment. Whatever the case may be, he doesn't deserve to be re-elected.

We have a spending problem.

Washington-speak is a language that is foreign to most taxpaying citizens, and unfortunately, the words and phrases our lawmakers use to communicate often hide the true meaning of what they are saying. Take the seemingly innocuous phrase "tax expenditure," for example. Ordinary people who are accustomed to words with common connotations interpret it to mean a government expenditure of our tax dollars to accomplish some goal, but they are wrong.

According to BusinessDictionary.com, a "tax expenditure" is "revenue a government foregoes through the provisions of tax laws that allow (1) deductions, exclusions, or exemptions from the taxpayers' taxable expenditure, income, or investment, (2) deferral of tax liability, or (3) preferential tax rates." This definition is accurate, but average taxpayers have never seen it and have no idea what it means.

In a 1999 Congressional report titled "Tax Expenditures: A Review and Analysis," the Joint Economic Study Committee said, "Tax expenditures are defined in the Congressional Budget Act of 1974 as 'revenue losses attributable to provisions of the Federal tax laws which allow a special exclusion, exemption, or deduction from gross income or which provide a special credit, a preferential rate of tax, or a deferral of tax liability.' Surrey himself stated that the tax expenditure budget is 'essentially an enumeration of the present tax incentives or tax subsidies, contained in our present income tax system.'"

In a nutshell, a "tax expenditure" is money that the government allows us to keep. The very existence of the phrase exposes an ugly truth. Our elected officials, Republicans and Democrats, think that we work for them, and out of the goodness of their hearts they permit us to keep a fraction of what we earn. The portion we keep is called a "tax expenditure."

I have followed politics closely for more than 40 years, and I have voted in every presidential election since 1968. While I taught at the University of Virginia, I served as Governor Chuck Robb's (D-Virginia) Policy Advisor for Regulatory Reform. Later, I was recruited by the Albemarle County Virginia Republican Party to run for the House of Delegates seat that George Allen (R-Virginia) vacated when he was elected to serve in the U.S. House of Representatives. I bring these things up merely to point out that my involvement in government and politics has not been cursory. Not once in my life have I heard a president or a candidate for the presidency use the phrase "tax expenditure" when addressing the American people—until Barack Obama.

In a budget speech delivered by Barack Obama during the summer of 2011, he said, "My budget calls for limiting itemized deductions for the wealthiest 2% of Americans – a reform that would reduce the deficit by $320 billion over ten years. But to reduce the deficit, I believe we should go further. That's why I'm calling on Congress to reform our individual tax code so that it is fair and simple – so that the amount of taxes you pay isn't determined by what kind of accountant you can afford. I believe reform should protect the middle class, promote economic growth, and build on the Fiscal Commission's model of reducing tax expenditures so that there is enough savings to both lower rates and lower the deficit. And as I called for in the State of the Union, we should reform our corporate tax code as well, to make our businesses and our economy more competitive."

People listening to the president's speech probably interpreted his remark about "reducing tax expenditures" to mean that he is in favor of cutting spending. Nothing could be further from the truth. What he said and what he meant is that he wants to eliminate some, if not all, of those pesky tax deductions that allow us to keep our hard-earned money and rob the government of the money it needs to pay for the programs that it deems worthy.

I did not read a single article in the mainstream media about President Obama's speech that addressed the "tax expenditure" issue. For that matter, I didn't hear or read about any Republican candidate for president or any Republican member of the House or Senate raising the "tax expenditure" issue in their analysis of his remarks, and this much is certain. Members of Congress know what a "tax expenditure" is.

There's a good reason why elected officials avoid using the phrase "tax expenditure" when talking with their constituents. If voters knew how people in Washington, Republicans and Democrats, really think, they would be appalled. We need fundamental philosophical change in Washington in both parties. It's time for our elected officials to realize that they work for us and not the other way around.

This is the bottom line. We don't have a tax revenue problem even though almost 50% of our fellow citizens pay no federal income taxes. We have a spending problem. If our elected officials don't get it or can't get it, then they shouldn't be in office. After 3 years in office, it's painfully obvious that President Obama doesn't get it.

Jobs, Jobs, Jobs: Where are they?

After a much publicized brouhaha over the scheduling of yet another "jobs speech" in September 2011, President Obama finally delivered an address to the nation in which he outlined one more stimulus program to create jobs. After all the hoopla and drama associated with the speech, investors expected something imaginative—something new, different, and better. Instead, the president tossed up a $450 billion package that looked eerily similar to the "stimulus" programs he sold to Congress in 2009, the ones that failed so miserably. Infrastructure spending, aid to states, high-speed rail, and temporary tax cuts highlighted the president's jobs proposal just like they did almost three years earlier.

It's not surprising that the Dow Jones Industrial Average dropped more than 300 points the day following the president's speech, or about 3%. Investors seemed to be saying, "Fool me once, shame on you. Fool me twice, shame on me." We've reached the point where Barack Obama isn't believable. Playing off Obama's campaign theme in 2008, I jokingly say, "I'm hoping for change now." But I'm not kidding. We need change, and if we don't get it, I'm afraid we're in for some tough times ahead—things that will make the last three years look like a cakewalk.

In his speech, Obama said, "There should be nothing controversial about this piece of legislation. Everything in here is the kind of proposal that's been supported by both Democrats and Republicans—including many who sit here tonight. And everything in this bill will be paid for. Everything."[7] It should come as no surprise that the president didn't explain how everything will be paid for.

Representative Paul Ryan (R-Wisconsin) gave a reasonable and accurate assessment of the president's proposal: "I didn't hear any new ideas. The only new idea from him that I was encouraged by is corporate tax reform. Broad based, lower rates. That's something we called for in our budget, we've always wanted to do. So perhaps some room for common ground there...I lost count of all the straw men up there. I mean, I was losing count at about 14 or 15. But we're used to hearing that. I think the last third of it was pretty much straw men...All the ideas in the front that he ticked off

---

[7] http://www.weeklystandard.com/blogs/obama-calls-450-billion-stimulus-speech-congress_592960.html

were the same things that he put in the stimulus that he proposed earlier, which are more Keynesian-style ideas that have already sort of proven to fail. I would rather we pass ideas that have proven to work rather than double down on ones that have proven to fail."[8]

Obviously, the president was under a lot of pressure after an August 2011 jobs report told the tale in no uncertain terms. Job growth in that month was zero, and the unemployment rate was stuck at a disturbingly high level—9.1%. The list of articles below appeared the day after the August 2011 jobs report was announced. They give you some idea about the mood of the country and about why the president was in such a rush to give his September jobs speech. To read the articles, simply google the titles.

- Zero Jobs 101 — the Psychology of Alienating Employers

- Obama admits his regulatory agenda is killing jobs

- Job growth stalls, fuels recession fears

- Zero Net Jobs Created in August

- Under the gun on jobs, Obama tells Congress to pass major transportation bill

- The Job Killer in Chief

- Obama Looking Like Job Killer In Chief

- Obama-Nomics: Half Full, Half Empty, or Just Half Assed?

Thinking people are increasingly skeptical about President Obama's intentions, his sincerity, his creativity, and some would argue, his intelligence. This is an example of what I mean. You'll recall that the president initially scheduled his September jobs speech to conflict with the Republican candidates' debate in South Carolina. That was a

---

[8] http://www.weeklystandard.com/blogs/house-republican-react-jobs-address_592970.html

major faux pas since he also wanted to deliver his address to a joint session of Congress. That would have ruled out attendance by some Republican candidates for president, and it would have pre-empted the Republican debate. That was a colossal blunder, and House Speaker John Boehner nixed the president's plan.

Next, the president tried to work in his speech around NFL games. It was a comical display of political ineptitude. Most people believed that the president simply wanted face time on national television (free advertising) with members of Congress dutifully sitting in front of him while he lectured them on what must be done. "Comical" is the wrong word. "Pathetic" is more like it because the president offered nothing new, nothing that even resembled an idea that has any chance of getting our economy moving again.

After the jobs speech, President Obama hit the road trying to sell his "new" plan to the American people. You can watch him doing it on a YouTube video titled "CNN— Barack Obama 'If you love me, you gotta help me pass this bill.'"[9] It demonstrates clearly what I've been saying in this book. Even though those shovel-ready programs that weren't shovel-ready in 2009 were still not shovel-ready in 2011, the president begged the overflow crowd to ignore reality and support him and his "new" plan. Why? It boiled down to one thing—ME. Obama invoked his "this is not about me" cliché as he always does, but we know when he says it that it's all about him. This time, Obama inserted a new phrase to encourage his adoring fans—"If you love me, you gotta help me pass this bill."

This isn't about love. It's about jobs, and President Obama's plan won't work this time any better than it worked the last time or the time before that. I like the way Senate minority leader Mitch McConnell (R-Kentucky) described the president's plan on *Meet the Press* September 18, 2011. He said, "There's little to be learned from the second kick of a mule." He's right, and the only people who haven't gotten the

---

[9] http://www.youtube.com/watch?v=V_NWzzD_e0Y

29

message are Obamanistas and the less than well-informed. Unfortunately, there are lots of them, so we have our work cut out for us. We need to educate ourselves and then we need to educate others or we will get four more years of Obama. Don't be complacent and let that happen.

A few days after he gave the jobs speech, President Obama hustled to the podium again to deliver another deficit speech. This is what David Brooks, a columnist for the *New York Times*, said about the president's deficit speech:

> "I'm a sap, a specific kind of sap. I'm an Obama Sap.
>
> When the president said the unemployed can't wait 14 more months for help and we had to do something right away, I believed him. When administration officials called around saying that the possibility of a double-dip recession was horrifyingly real and that it would be irresponsible not to come up with a package that could pass right away, I believed them.
>
> I liked Obama's payroll tax cut ideas and urged Republicans to play along. But of course I'm a sap. When the president unveiled the second half of his stimulus it became clear that this package has nothing to do with helping people right away or averting a double dip. This is a campaign marker, not a jobs bill.
>
> It recycles ideas that couldn't get passed even when Democrats controlled Congress."[10]

Brooks was correct. The president just rehashed the same old same old.[11] Generally speaking, the left loved the president's deficit speech because it was laced with "tax the rich" invective, and the right hated it for the same reason. [12] But, and this

---

[10] http://www.nytimes.com/2011/09/20/opinion/brooks-obama-rejects-obamaism.html?_r=1

[11] http://www.theatlantic.com/politics/archive/2011/09/same-old-tax-fight/245316/

[12] http://www.weeklystandard.com/blogs/obama-its-not-class-warfare-its-math_593709.html

is a big but, liberal Democratic Senator Chuck Schumer (D-New York), didn't like it at all.[13] The tax hikes that the president kept saying were essential were too liberal for him, and that's saying a lot.

The president said that his deficit proposal was based on simple math.[14] The simple part was correct, but the math part wasn't. The political math is taking shape, and Obama's tax and spend approach is becoming less popular every day as voters are coming to terms with stark reality.

Thankfully, every House member and one-third of the Senate faces re-election in 2012. Keep in mind that in 2009 a heavily Democratic Congress gave the president carte blanche to deal with our nation's economic woes. The Troubled Asset Relief Program (TARP) and other stimulus programs that cost American taxpayers close to $2 trillion[15] were supposed to revitalize the economy and keep the unemployment rate below 8%, but they were designed by President Obama to achieve his objectives, not ours. People who were hoping for change when they voted for Obama were disheartened because what they got was the largest and most expensive boondoggle in American history. The change that President Obama had in mind was even more taxing and spending— more than thinking people dreamed possible.

In 2010, Democrats took a shellacking at the polls precisely because the president didn't deliver on his oft-repeated promises. In September 2011 as the 2012 campaign was getting underway in earnest, the president stood in front of Congress again and told them and the American people that after weeks of thinking about what needs to be done he had nothing new to say. Then he offered up his woefully lacking deficit plan

---

[13] http://www.weeklystandard.com/blogs/obamas-tax-hike-too-liberal-new-york-says-chuck-schumer_593716.html

[14] http://www.theatlanticwire.com/politics/2011/09/obama-gets-feisty-not-class-warfare-its-math/42658/

[15] http://gigaom.com/cleantech/ge-looking-to-tap-2-trillion-of-stimulus-spending/

again. At the same time, he pressured Israel to make concessions to the Palestinians that she should not make.

As a result, in mid-September 2011 a Republican won the New York House seat vacated by Representative Anthony Weiner after he became involved in a lurid photo and email scandal. That was unheard of if not unprecedented, and the Democratic loser, David Weprin, blamed President Obama.[16] That seat had been held by a Democrat for more than 80 years, since before the Great Depression, and the people of New York's heavily Democratic 9th congressional district handed it to a Republican because they were fed up with Obama.

In October 2011, Obama's political game playing continued while our economy crumbled. In an article for *American Thinker*,[17] I pointed out that Senate Democrats didn't even take up[18] the president's "jobs plan" until they and the president became the target of ridicule for their lack of performance on the jobs front. Even so, demonstrating how out of touch Democrats are, Senate Majority Leader Harry Reid (D-Nevada) moved "to block[19] Senate Minority Leader Mitch McConnell's attempt to bring the 'jobs' bill up for a vote in the Senate." But that's not all. Senate Democrats tacked onto the "jobs" bill a "millionaires' tax," and Reid rewrote[20] Senate rules making it very difficult for the minority party to force the majority party to take uncomfortable votes. If that's not political game playing, I don't know what is.

---

[16] http://www.reuters.com/article/2011/09/15/us-usa-congress-weiner-idUSTRE78E7CY20110915

[17] http://www.americanthinker.com/blog/2011/10/the_skunk_tells_the_hound_that_he_stinks.html

[18] http://www.politico.com/news/stories/1011/65026.html

[19] http://thehill.com/blogs/floor-action/senate/185455-reid-blocks-mcconnells-call-for-an-immediate-vote-on-obamas-jobs-plan

[20] http://campaign2012.washingtonexaminer.com/blogs/beltway-confidential/reid-rewrites-senate-rules-shocking-move?utm_source=10/6%20special%20update%20Washington%20Examiner%20Opinion%20-%2010/06/2011&utm_medium=email&utm_campaign=Washington%20Examiner:%20Opin

Making the charade even more surreal, Obama took to the airwaves[21] again the very next day and blamed Republicans for standing in the way of progress. He even attacked "Mitch McConnell several times by name, without ever acknowledging the real reason his legislation has stalled in the upper chamber: Democratic opposition."[22]

This is the bottom line. The unemployment rate in the United States is unacceptably high, and the economy is moving in the wrong direction. The president's jobs speech and his deficit speech and the other speeches he has made have done nothing to encourage thinking people in the Republican Party or the Democratic Party, and they have reinforced the belief among Obama's political opponents that he is an uninspiring president, at best. We don't need more speeches. We need a president who is serious about creating jobs.

President Obama's performance record offers little hope for the future, but it screams that real change is desperately needed. This is what the president actually did during his first 3 years in office:

1. He increased regulations with reckless abandon in virtually every sector of the economy while he had veto-proof majorities in the House and Senate.

2. He maneuvered the federal government into position to exert control over the United States healthcare industry, the energy sector of the economy, and the US auto industry, for example. His unprecedented intrusions into the private sector of the economy produced results that were dismal, but he refuses to admit that his approach is fatally flawed. Nothing can convince him that he is wrong—not even hard data.

---

[21] http://townhall.com/tipsheet/guybenson/2011/10/06/awful_evaluating_obamas_re-run_press_conference

[22] http://townhall.com/tipsheet/guybenson/2011/10/04/heh_reid_blocks_senate_vote_on_obamas__jobs_bill

3. In 2010, when Republicans took control of the House of Representative and Democrats in the Senate lost their veto-proof majority, President Obama resorted to ruling by fiat. If he couldn't win Congressional support for his initiatives, he bypassed Congress altogether and issued executive orders to accomplish his objectives. As peculiar as this may sound to most Americans, the Obama presidency is as close to a dictatorship as we have seen since the Civil War when President Abraham Lincoln suspended habeas corpus.

4. The Dodd-Frank financial reform package was supposed to prevent the kinds of abuses that led to the housing bubble and its eventual collapse. When he signed the legislation in July 2010, President Obama said, "Passing this bill was no easy task. To get there, we had to overcome the furious lobbying of an array of powerful interest groups and a partisan minority determined to block change. So the members who are here today, both on the stage and in the audience, they have done a great service in devoting so much time and expertise to this effort, to looking out for the public interests and not the special interests."[23]

As it turned out, Dodd-Frank was wildly unpopular on Wall Street and Main Street. It had the effect of restricting credit to even the most creditworthy borrowers. As of September 2011, creditworthy small business borrowers still face a mountain of paperwork if they need loans to run their businesses.

Making matters worse, the two members of Congress for whom the bill was named—Senator Chris Dodd (D-Connecticut) and Representative Barney Frank (D-Massachusetts)—are deeply embroiled in controversies over their complicity in creating the housing problems in the first place. Additionally,

---

[23] http://www.whitehouse.gov/blog/2010/07/21/president-obama-signs-wall-street-reform-no-easy-task

Senator Dodd received sweetheart loans[24] from Countrywide—a mortgage company that was implicated in a multitude of mortgage abuses, and Representative Frank was under the gun for an alleged conflict of interest[25] involving his boyfriend Herb Moses who was Fannie Mae's assistant director for product initiatives.

Fannie Mae is a quasigovernment organization that was created during the Great Depression to expand the secondary mortgage market and to securitize mortgage-backed securities. To this day, Dodd-Frank remains one of the most troublesome obstacles in the path of recovery for the housing industry, and the United States economy will not recover until the housing industry recovers.

5. "Deficits and Debt Gone Wild" should be the tagline of the Obama presidency. Nothing he has done as president suggests that he has even a smidgen of economic sense. His speeches do little to hide that fact. Where the economy is concerned, Barack Obama is totally out of his element.

6. Despite what he says, President Obama must have believed that the Great Recession wasn't such a big deal because he used most of the money he was given by Congress in TARP and other stimulus programs to reward individuals and groups that supported his candidacy for president in 2008—especially unions. The result has been a predictable backlash[26] against unions in general and government unions in particular.

---

[24] http://www.portfolio.com/news-markets/top-5/2008/06/12/Countrywide-Loan-Scandal/

[25] http://www.foxnews.com/story/0,2933,432501,00.html

[26] http://www.weeklystandard.com/blogs/gallup-union-approval-near-record-lows_592110.html

In state after state, governors have gone to war with government employee unions because they have to balance their budgets. Their constitutions require it, but at the federal level under President Obama, we just keep printing money as if it doesn't matter. The result has been just what you would expect. According to columnist Austin Hill, "After almost three years of 'transforming'—which has involved putting healthcare under government control, a government take-over of two car companies, huge expansions in government control over banking and lending institutions, hundreds of millions of dollars spent to create 'green jobs,' and a roughly 30% increase in government spending overall—nobody seems happy with the results (not even the president himself)."[27] No one is happy because nothing the president has done makes economic sense.

7. President Obama continues to vilify the rich who he says pay too little tax, and he is trying to position himself as the champion of the poor who he says pay too much tax. The statistics I presented earlier prove that argument is baloney. The rich pay for everything we do as a nation, and the poor pay nothing. When roughly 50% of the population pays no federal income tax and about 40% of the population gets more back from the government than they pay in taxes, you know beyond any reasonable doubt that the poor aren't the only people who pay no federal income tax. The data points to an irrefutable truth. The United States is becoming a socialist country, and under President Obama the speed of change is accelerating. So this is the question we have to answer. Do we want to be a socialist country? If the answer is "no," then Barack Obama should not be re-elected.

Despite all the evidence, President Obama seems determined to make fairness in our tax system[28] the primary issue in the 2012 election. He's right about the fairness

---

[27]

http://townhall.com/columnists/austinhill/2011/09/04/obama,_phd%E2%80%99s,_and_some_bizarre_ideas_abo ut_labor

[28] http://townhall.com/columnists/johncgoodman/2011/09/03/the_next_election_will_be_about_taxes

issue, but he is totally off base when he points his finger at the rich. Our problem isn't that the rich pay too little tax. Our problem is that we spend too much money at the federal level of government and approximately half of our citizens pay no federal income tax. This isn't rocket science, but it's too much for the president to grasp.

If things continue as they are, it's just a matter of time before our fiscal house of cards collapses just like the housing market did. The Standard & Poor's downgrade of United States bonds was a shot across the bow. Unfortunately, President Obama didn't get that message either. He has done more to destroy our economy than any of his predecessors. Donald Trump said that Barack Obama is the worst president in the history of the United States. Mountains of evidence support that conclusion.

An Interesting but True Anecdote

My wife, Katie, and I rode out Hurricane Irene in August 2011 in Massachusetts. We lost electricity for several hours, and that opened the door for playing board games that we played as kids. Our niece, Danielle, wanted to play the new version of Monopoly—the electronic version. I enjoyed the game as a boy so that sounded like a good idea.

The electronic version of Monopoly is very different from the game I knew. For instance, it doesn't have paper money; it uses something that resembles a credit card instead; the names of properties have changed almost completely and so have their prices; and the Monopoly economy has been inflated beyond recognition.

While we were playing, it dawned on me that President Obama must have learned about business and government by playing electronic Monopoly. My first clue came when I passed "Go." You get $2,000,000 for passing "Go." When I was a kid, you got $200 for passing "Go." I thought, *In Obama's world, everyone should be a millionaire, and no one should be required to earn anything—except in sports…maybe, so this is where he must have developed that philosophy.*

My next clue came when one of our players found herself in financial difficulty. She should have been required to sell property to raise the capital she needed to pay her expenses. Instead, we voted to give each player an additional $5,000,000. I voted against it, but I lost. The payout solved her immediate problem, but it inflated the economy for everyone.

A few turns later, Danielle needed a piece of property that was owned by the player who was in dire financial straits, so Danielle made a deal with her to buy it. Problem is the other player didn't take into account the inflated value of everything, and she sold it to Danielle for just 20% more than she paid for it. The other player thought she was making a great deal, but I told her that it wasn't a good deal as forcefully as I could without being offensive. I explained that owning her property would enable Danielle to build houses and hotels on all three properties in the group. Danielle could wipe her out if she was unfortunate enough to land on any one of those properties. The deal went through anyway, and we continued playing.

Within a few turns, Danielle needed a piece of property that I owned, so I decided to negotiate. I already owned one airport, and Danielle owned two of them. In the modern version of Monopoly, airports have taken the place of railroads, and the payoff for owning several of them is huge. I told Danielle that I would sell her the piece of property she needed in return for both of her airports plus $5,000,000. Since the property cost me only $2,000,000, Danielle rejected my offer, but I knew she would need it later so I didn't budge.

It didn't take long for Danielle to realize that she needed my property no matter what the price. She was on the verge of closing a deal with me when we got hungry and decided to take a break. While we were eating, I thought about it and became even more convinced that President Obama learned about business and government by playing electronic Monopoly. Here's why:

1. No one is required to accomplish anything to become a millionaire. You're entitled to be rich because you occupy a seat at the table. Does that sound familiar?

2. When difficulties arise, the solution is to dole out money with no strings attached. How is that different from Obama administration policies?

3. Debt is not an issue. Does anyone honestly believe that President Obama has a clue how much trouble we are in as a nation because of our horrendous debt load? I'll be blunt. If he does, then he is purposely trying to bankrupt this country.

Monopoly is not the real world. I wish our president understood that. Thankfully, we never went back to the Monopoly game. When we finished eating, we decided to play Trivial Pursuit instead. Voting President Obama out of office may not be that easy, but it can be done.

A Gallup poll[29] taken in late September 2011 revealed that for the first time the majority of Americans are beginning to realize that President Obama is responsible for our nation's economic woes. Reading this book and telling others about it will help to educate even more of them. It's essential for people to understand the facts.

---

[29] http://www.weeklystandard.com/blogs/gallup-first-time-majority-americans-blame-obama-economy_594010.html

Chapter 3

The Economy in Light of Obamacare: Unnecessary Uncertainty

Businesspeople are reluctant to invest in an uncertain environment, and Obamacare is a huge question mark in the minds of business men and women who, unlike the federal government, must make ends meet. The global economic outlook is uncertain at best. Sovereign debt issues in Europe and other parts of the world, war and peace issues in the Middle East, and deficit and debt problems in the United States have created lots of unanswered questions for businesspeople to think about. Adding Obamacare to the mix only makes things worse because no one, not even the president, has been able to come up with a good estimate of its cost. As long as there remains a cloud of uncertainty about the cost of Obamacare, the United States economy will suffer.

4 Problems with Obamacare

The problems with Obamacare are many and varied. According to Dr. Marc Siegel, an associate professor of medicine at New York University's Langone Medical Center, it has 4 essential problems. Even Dr. Howard Dean—an internist, a Democratic candidate for the presidency in 2004, and past head of the Democratic National Committee—predicts[30] that eventually the mandate provision in Obamacare will be dropped either because it's unconstitutional or because people reject it. Siegel believes the mandate provision is the first essential problem with Obamacare.

---

[30] http://firstread.msnbc.msn.com/_news/2010/08/06/4832127-dean-predicts-demise-of-insurance-mandate

The federal government can't require United States citizens to purchase a product—any product—because it's unconstitutional. States can. For example, states can require their citizens to purchase car insurance without violating the Constitution. Most states have done just that and have encountered no constitutional problems. Similarly, Massachusetts implemented a mandated healthcare plan that's similar to Obamacare and didn't run afoul of the Constitution. Other states can do the same thing if they so choose, but the federal government is not allowed to cross that constitutional barrier. The mandate issue will contribute to the fog surrounding Obamacare until the United States Supreme Court finally drives a stake through its heart by declaring it unconstitutional and, for all practical purposes, dead.

Second, Siegel points to the growing doctor shortage[31] in the United States and says, "Many of us who are practicing medicine in the current climate are not happy with third party payers of any kind, public or private, and we are dropping out of insurance, and beginning to band together to protest."[32] The US doctor shortage is real and serious, and it's getting worse. Rural areas[33] are especially hard-hit by the doctor shortage since most physicians prefer to practice in metropolitan areas.

Siegel's second point is an economic argument against Obamacare. The president's plan mandates health insurance and will unquestionably drive up demand for medical care. But the number of doctors is relatively fixed in the short-term, and long-term growth in the number of doctors will be slow. The effect of increasing the demand for medical services faster than the increase in the supply of doctors will inevitably lead to higher prices, price controls, and/or rationing. For these reasons, a strong argument can be made that Obamacare won't bring down the cost of medical

---

[31] http://online.wsj.com/article/SB10001424052702304506904575180331528424238.html

[32] http://www.foxnews.com/opinion/2010/08/09/dr-marc-siegel-obamacare-physicians-howard-dean-mandate-health-insurance-care/

[33] http://seattletimes.nwsource.com/html/health/2009078934_ruraldocs18m0.html

care in the United States as we were told by the president. In fact, it will do just the opposite, and on top of that, it will result in rationing of medical care and "death panels"[34] that will have the power to determine which patients should be treated. Neither of these outcomes is popular with the electorate, and the very idea of "death panels" is appalling to the American people for obvious reasons.

Third, Siegel believes that the president's assumption about the extent to which medical patients will use hospital emergency rooms after implementation of Obamacare is wrong. Currently, people who have no insurance can receive treatment in emergency rooms because emergency rooms can't turn patients away.[35] Emergency room treatment is very expensive, and it drives up the cost of medical care for everyone. If Obama's assumption proves to be invalid, then the logic for Obamacare breaks down completely. At this time, the effect of Obamacare on emergency room usage is anyone's guess. As a practicing physician, Siegel's opinion should be taken seriously, and he is not alone. Many other doctors agree with him.

Finally, Siegel says that Obamacare supporters have failed to consider "how advancing technologies, which are expensive, targeted, and personalized, are going to be covered by a one-size-fits all insurance model that has no disincentive for overuse and so can only control premiums by denying services."[36] He's right, and I would add this. Everything about Obamacare is based on assumptions which if proven to be false mean that Obamacare is little more than a pig in a poke. That's why many opponents of Obamacare believe the president's real goal is to transform the United States into a socialist country. Since healthcare accounts for roughly 18% of the US economy, government control of healthcare is a good place to start the transformation process. I won't address President Obama's "true intentions" in this book because I'm not a

---

[34] http://spectator.org/blog/2010/12/27/the-inevitability-of-death-pan

[35] http://www.tennhelp.com/Library/Documents/1150904389.52/ERcardweb_705.pdf

[36] http://www.foxnews.com/opinion/2010/08/09/dr-marc-siegel-obamacare-physicians-howard-dean-mandate-health-insurance-care/

psychoanalyst, but I will say this. People who question the president's ulterior motives aren't being foolish.

Obamacare is Worse than You Think

Several months after President Obama signed Obamacare into law, a *Washington Examiner*[37] editorial pointed out several other salient problems with the plan:

1. According to actuaries for Medicare, it will increase costs for the government, and it's likely to increase the cost for privately funded healthcare as well.

2. Despite Obama's assurances to the contrary, Obamacare covers elective abortions. That assurance was needed to win passage of the legislation because many millions of Americans oppose abortion on demand for moral reasons.

3. The president's own estimates suggest that "as many as 69 percent of employees, 80 percent of small businesses, and 64 percent of large businesses will be forced to change coverage, probably to more expensive plans" as a result of Obamacare.

4. Obamacare will increase the cost of health insurance overall from "1 to 9 percent" because of the provision that requires insurers to cover their clients' children until they are 26 years old.

5. As a result of Obamacare, seasonal employers in the ski and amusement park industries, for example, will have "to pay huge fines, cut hours, or lay off employees."

6. Obamacare requires states to guarantee treatment and payment for indigent Medicaid recipients—patients that many doctors refuse to treat since they

---

[37] http://washingtonexaminer.com/opinion/examiner-editorial-obamacare-even-worse-critics-thought

lose money each time they treat a Medicaid patient. States that are already reeling from massive budget shortfalls can ill afford to foot that bill.

7. The nonmedical tax compliance cost for small businesses under Obamacare will be enormous, thus forcing them to increase prices for the goods and services they sell. The effect on inflation could be dramatic.

8. "Obamacare allows the IRS to confiscate part or all of your tax refund if you do not purchase a qualified insurance plan," and it increases the number of IRS agents to make sure that people toe the line. Some argue that Obamacare is movement toward a police state for that reason. Again, while I don't know the president's "true intentions," I will say that questions along those lines are not off-the-wall.

Many Questions Remain Unanswered

Several of these problems have been addressed to some degree and others have not, but to this day no one, and I mean no one, knows for sure what Obamacare is, what it will become, and what it will cost. Since passage of Obamacare, the Obama administration has issued more than 1300[38] waivers and exemptions, and that number keeps rising almost daily. More than half[39] of the Obamacare waivers so far have gone to union members. That should surprise no one since President Obama has given unions preferential treatment since the day he took office. All these facts about Obamacare lead to several inescapable conclusions:

1. Obama's strategy for winning voter support for his plan is to exempt groups from Obamacare's provisions if they scream loudly enough.

---

[38] http://dailycaller.com/2011/05/19/obamacare-transparency-fail-who%E2%80%99s-still-waiting-for-waivers-and-who-got-denied-obama-won%E2%80%99t-tell-us/

[39] http://www.weeklystandard.com/blogs/over-half-all-obamacare-waivers-given-union-members_561115.html

2. Because of their favorable treatment, union members will not pay their fair share of Obamacare expenses thus forcing nonunion workers to pay a disproportionate share of the cost.

3. According to the Congressional Budget Office, Obamacare will increase the national debt by $226 billion[40] before the end of 2019.

4. The fog surrounding Obamacare is getting thicker by the day.

5. Economic uncertainty where Obamacare is concerned is forcing businesses, both small and large, to hold back on making investments that would create jobs.

The problems with Obamacare were known by the President well in advance of its passage by Congress, even though Congress itself was unaware of most of them because of the way the bill was handled by Senate Majority Leader Harry Reid and House Speaker Nancy Pelosi. When Pelosi told reporters that Congress would learn what was in the bill when they saw it, she wasn't kidding. Members of the Senate and the House were clueless by design. As of September 2011, Obamacare remains a mystery. The cost to the US economy is huge, and American workers are paying a high price as well because prudent business men and women won't make investments that lead to job creation until they have a handle on costs.

Some have argued[41] persuasively that uncertainty surrounding Obamacare contributed to the Standard & Poor's downgrade of US bonds. That may be conjecture, but this much is certain. The unwillingness of Congress and the Obama administration to come to grips with the rapidly increasing costs of federal government programs did lead to the downgrade, and Obamacare will increase costs at the federal level. The only question is "by how much?"

---

[40] http://www.weeklystandard.com/blogs/cbo-obamacare-would-increase-national-debt-spend-medicare-savings_536716.html

[41] http://hotair.com/archives/2011/08/07/was-the-downgrade-a-rejection-of-obamacare/

Chapter 4

"Oh what a tangled web we weave, when first we practise to deceive!"

If I were still teaching strategy full-time, I would require my students to watch *Too Big to Fail*, and I would devote 2 class periods to it. It's a recent movie that is as enlightening as any movie I've seen in a while.

In the first class, we would talk about what happens when do-gooders in Washington decide that government can do the impossible—things like trying to make homeownership a virtual entitlement. In the second class, we would examine what happens when government severely limits its options by taking on mountains of debt that it can ill afford to repay. At the end of those classes, even diehard liberal progressives would have to admit that there are serious limitations to what government can accomplish.

Saying that our government has overreached is an understatement. From welfare to Medicaid to food stamps to Medicare to Social Security to Obamacare to ill-conceived subsidies of various sorts, our government has made promises that we can't fulfill even if we raise tax rates to the stratosphere. Every government program has a constituency and subsidies have staying power even if they make no sense. There isn't any way for us to solve the deficit and debt problems we face as a nation unless we scale back those promises. Pretending otherwise is foolish and dangerous.

Social Security is a perfect example of government gone crazy. It was created during the Great Depression to provide income security for retired American workers. Early recipients of Social Security benefits faced no problems because there were many workers per retiree. In 1945, for instance, there were 41.9[42] workers per Social Security recipient, but by September 2011, there were only 1.75[43] workers per retiree. While the number of workers per retiree declined, new features were added to the program, and in the 1970s under President Nixon, Social Security benefits were tied to inflation. Automatic cost of living adjustments (COLAs) took Social Security spending decisions out of the hands of Congress, and Social Security costs spiraled out of control. Social Security is a classic example of government overreach, but there are many other government programs with similar difficulties. Each one of them contributes to our deficit and debt problems.

Nothing has been done to deal with the problems in Social Security. That's what led Texas Governor Rick Perry, a Republican candidate for the presidency, to call Social Security a Ponzi scheme.[44] It's not a Ponzi scheme in the technical sense, but it is seriously underfunded. Unfunded liabilities associated with Social Security amount to just under $18 trillion.[45] It's obvious that we have made promises we can't keep where Social Security is concerned, and the program needs a complete overhaul. That's something Barack Obama and his liberal progressive comrades in the House and Senate have been unwilling to do. The mere mention of Social Security sends them into a furious demagogic rage. This can't continue.

There once was a time when US leaders lectured third world countries about the idiocy of taking on debt without regard for consequences. Now they are returning the

---

[42] http://www.cnsnews.com/news/article/labor-dept-data-only-175-full-time-private-sector-workers-social-security-recipient

[43] http://www.cnsnews.com/news/article/labor-dept-data-only-175-full-time-private-sector-workers-social-security-recipient

[44] http://www.cbsnews.com/8301-503544_162-20098635-503544.html

[45] http://www.forbes.com/2009/05/14/taxes-social-security-opinions-columnists-medicare.html

favor because what we've done makes what they did look pale by comparison. We've turned the world's largest creditor nation into the largest debtor nation in the history of the world in three short decades, and it's time to face the facts.

Conservatives in the House of Representatives have made a good start at getting our financial house in order. Predictably, they're being demonized by liberal progressives in Congress, but this much is certain. We must solve our deficit and debt problems, and time is of the essence. Political brinksmanship may be the currency of the realm in Washington, but mistakes at this critical juncture can be very costly. They might even mean the fiscal collapse of our nation. Are our political leaders so thoughtless that they would gamble on that possibility? I hope not, but judging by Barack Obama's performance as president, I wouldn't bet on it.

There is plenty of blame to go around. Democrats and Republicans share responsibility for our financial crisis, so playing the blame game is pointless. This is not about political parties, and it's not about haves and have-nots. It's about averting a looming financial catastrophe that will affect every one of us unless the problem is solved. Young and old, rich and poor, all of us have a stake in the outcome. Is the political class up to the challenge? In the House of Representatives, the answer is "yes." In the Senate and the White House, the answer is "no."

The Tea Party Didn't Cause the Standard & Poor's Downgrade

Senator John Kerry[46] from Massachusetts blames the Tea Party for the Standard & Poor's downgrade. He says that Senate Republicans won't even consider raising taxes because of Tea Party influence. David Axelrod,[47] President Obama's close personal

---

[46] http://thehill.com/homenews/senate/175801-kerry-blames-tea-party-for-downgrade-says-senate-gop-willing-to-raise-taxes

[47] http://finance.townhall.com/columnists/johnransom/2011/08/08/shocker_axelrod_blames_the_tea_party

friend and advisor, says the same thing. That Kerry and Axelrod would blame the Tea Party isn't surprising. That they have the unmitigated gall to ignore their role in helping to create this mess is.

Of all the people in the Senate today, John Kerry stands out in my mind as the epitome of liberal progressivism. For instance, he harps on the need to control carbon emissions, but he jets from one of his many houses[48] to another. Similarly, despite his rhetoric about carbon emissions, he has an SUV[49]—something that's abhorrent to environmentalists. Kerry's exploits in Vietnam gained him national recognition when he lied[50] to Congress about the conduct of the war. He once was a prosecutor, but his performance record[51] was very poor, so poor in fact that I hesitate to call it a "performance" record. The words "John Kerry" and "truth" shouldn't be used in the same sentence, and "truth" seems to be a foreign concept to most liberal progressives—including President Obama.

When Senator Kerry blames the Tea Party for the debt downgrade, he's really saying that they prevented the Senate from moving ahead willy-nilly with their tax and spend solutions to every problem we face with the full support of President Obama. Today, Democrats in the Senate are a huge part of our problem. They're a problem in the House too, but they are in the minority there. After the November 2012 election, hopefully they'll be in the minority in the Senate as well.

David Axelrod made a fortune by cozying up to people with political power or politicians on the come. Barack Obama is his trophy catch. Axelrod's game is politics. That's all he knows. His opinion about the economy should carry about as much

---

[48] http://www.snopes.com/politics/kerry/homes.asp

[49] http://www.democraticunderground.com/discuss/duboard.php?az=view_all&address=115x7823

[50] http://www.militarycorruption.com/kerry4.htm

[51] http://www.freerepublic.com/focus/f-news/1256581/posts

weight as my dog's views, but you could say the same thing about the president. That's the nature of our democratic republic. Sometimes we elect ignoramuses to high offices, and they surround themselves with people who make them look good by comparison.

I'm not a Republican or a Democrat. I'm not a Tea Partier, either. I'm just a concerned citizen who looks at the facts and draws conclusions. The facts tell me that this nation is on a collision course with financial disaster, that we tax and spend too much, and that the electorate has been far too patient with our political leaders for far too long. The facts also tell me that the Tea Party is the group most responsible for the recent change in the status quo in Washington, and the Tea Party supports conservative candidates.

Republicans have interpreted the tea leaves correctly. They know that the tide has shifted. Liberal progressives in the Democratic Party still hold sway, and they stubbornly refuse to admit that the electorate has had enough of their nonsense. Their intransigence has already cost them the House of Representatives. It's going to cost them even more if they don't change their ways.

The Standard & Poor's downgrade of US bonds was based on one thing. As a nation we spend more than we are willing to pay for. As a result, we have taken on too much debt. The Tea Party didn't cause that problem. In fact, they're trying to solve it. "More of the same" liberal progressive politicians like John Kerry and liberal progressive mouthpieces like David Axelrod are the ones who got us into this mess, and they don't have any idea how to get us out of it. They and people of their ilk are responsible for this mess. Blaming Standard & Poor's or the Tea Party for our fiscal insanity is like blaming the thermometer for telling you that you have a fever.

Obama's Plan: Shoot the Messenger

There is no question that Obama administration policies have contributed greatly to our deficit and debt problems. Even so, President Obama was all upset because Standard & Poor's downgraded[52] US bonds from AAA to AA+. But Standard & Poor's isn't the only one sounding the alarm. China holds about $1 trillion of our roughly $14.5 trillion debt, and Chinese leaders blasted the US for gross mismanagement, a bloated welfare system, and too much defense spending. They demanded that Washington solve our financial problems to protect their dollar investments. You can't blame them. You would be concerned too if you owned US bonds.

Before the downgrade was announced publicly, Standard & Poor's notified the Obama administration that it was coming. That got people in the Treasury Department working, not to solve the problem mind you. They were working to prove that Standard & Poor's made an error. There was a $2 trillion mistake in Standard & Poor's math, and people at the Treasury Department used that fact to try and shame Standard & Poor's into not going ahead with the downgrade even though they had warned the feds during the debt ceiling debate that they expected at least $4 trillion in budget cuts and/or revenue increases.

Congress didn't even come close to that number as I pointed out in chapter 2, yet President Obama applauded the debt ceiling compromise as though it was a giant leap forward. He couldn't have been more mistaken. The brouhaha in Congress over the debt ceiling produced a bill that was supposed to have these features:

- A $38.5 billion spending cut in 2011.

---

[52] http://abcnews.go.com/Business/us-expecting-standard-poors-debt-rating-downgrade-government/story?id=14220820

- A $917 billion reduction in spending over the next 10 years, only it was a cut in the rate of spending growth over the next 10 years—not a cut in spending.

- A cut in spending next year of $22 billion out of a $3.6 trillion budget. That's a cut of roughly .05%. That's half a penny out of every spending dollar.

- A super-committee of Congress composed of members of the House and the Senate is supposed to come up with another $1.5 trillion in budget cuts or tax increases by Thanksgiving. Whatever the super-committee comes up with will get a simple up-or-down vote in both houses of Congress. There will be no amendments.

Entitlement spending wasn't even touched, and that's the biggest problem we face. It's the problem that can and will bankrupt this nation unless we do something about it. Even so, speaking about the bill, President Obama said, "This process has been messy. It's taken far too long. Nevertheless, ultimately, the leaders of both parties have found their way toward compromise, and I want to thank them for that. (The deal) will allow us to avoid default and end the crisis that Washington imposed on the rest of America. It ensures also that we will not face this same kind of crisis again in six months, or eight months, or 12 months. And it will begin to lift the cloud of debt and the cloud of uncertainty that hangs over our economy."[53]

For President Obama, the most important thing about the debt ceiling deal was that it eliminated the possibility that there will be another battle in Congress over raising the debt ceiling during the 2012 election. That may be a token victory since voters are more tuned in to our deficit and debt problems now than they have ever been. They are beginning to realize that we spend too much, that we tax too much, that we have mortgaged our futures, and that we've made promises we can't keep.

---

[53] http://www.washingtonpost.com/politics/debt-ceiling-deal-reached-between-obama-and-congress-sorting-out-the-winners-and-losers/2011/08/01/gIQAC9R4nI_story.html?wprss=rss_whitehouse

Voters are also waking up to Washington budget chicanery, and the debt ceiling compromise was long on hyperbole and short on quantifiable results. As I said in chapter 2, instead of cutting spending by $38.5 billion in 2011 as we were told by President Obama, House Speaker Boehner, and Majority Leader Reid, the actual spending reduction amounted to only about $352 million in 2011. That's a mere pittance, less than a rounding error, and it didn't offer much hope that the United States was changing the deficit and debt trajectory—something Standard & Poor's was looking for. That's what prompted the US bond downgrade.

If President Obama's grand vision for America was a new idea, a potentially better idea, that would be one thing, but it's not. He wants to overlay the typical socialist state model on our system, and socialism has a proven record of failure. It caused the Soviet Union to collapse, and today Italy, Spain, Greece, and Ireland to name just a few European countries are reeling under the weight of socialism. The only thing that's new about Obama's plan is his determination to impose it on us against our will. The Chinese are moving away from traditional socialism as fast as they can because they have firsthand experience with it, and they know that it doesn't work. That should tell us something.

Our system is tottering as well. Not only do we spend too much money, but as I have pointed out already, half of our population pays no federal income taxes. They freeload off people who do pay taxes. The wealthy among us, people that the Obamanistas like to blame for our fiscal problems, pay for almost everything we do as a nation, and the president thinks they should pay more. The scary part is that we've promised to spend so much more money in the future that the wealthy don't have enough resources to pay for all the promises we've made.

If you add up all the changes that President Obama has proposed to increase our tax revenue including eliminating the Bush tax cuts, cutting oil subsidies, and wiping out the tax breaks for people who own private jets, for example, we would still have a serious fiscal problem. Rep. Paul Ryan (R-WI) introduced a sensible plan in the House and so did President Obama's National Commission on Fiscal Responsibility and Reform, but he flatly rejected both of them. Rating agencies would be derelict in their duties if they didn't send us strong signals before we reach the tipping point, or the point of no return.

Interestingly, rating agencies as a group came under fire for not doing their jobs in a professional manner when they rated those so-called "investment grade securities" made up of US-backed mortgage securities that Wall Street bundled and sold to the world, thus precipitating the housing collapse and the Great Recession. Rather than complaining about the Standard & Poor's downgrade, the feds should be thanking them for telling us the truth and hopefully for getting Congress off its derriere.

President Obama lives in a make-believe world where up is down and right is wrong. Nothing you hear coming out of the White House or the Treasury Department makes any sense. The same is true for the Justice Department, the National Labor Relations Board (NLRB), and the Environmental Protection Agency (EPA) to name just a few. The Standard & Poor's downgrade has made the Obamanistas scramble. That's something the electorate has been unable to accomplish. Even after the 2010 mid-term shellacking that Obama took, he stayed the course. The message needs to be much clearer in 2012.

The arrogance of President Obama and his underlings is breathtaking. They can't accept the fact that there is even a slight possibility that they might be wrong. From their perspective, the unwashed masses, people like you and me, are either out of touch or just plain stupid. They are wrong, and thanks to the Standard & Poor's downgrade, the truth is finally getting out.

Trying to Hide the Truth by Mixing Energy Policy and Fiscal Policy

As the economy was slumping in June 2011, the International Energy Agency announced that it would make 60 million barrels of oil[54] from global strategic stockpiles available to the market. Most of it came from the US Strategic Petroleum Reserve (SPR). That may have sounded like a good idea, but it wasn't. It showed how desperate President Obama was to make it look as though he was doing something to stimulate the economy.

The SPR is supposed to be available in case of an emergency. There was no emergency, so why was the oil released? There is only one logical answer. President Obama was trying to stave off criticism and improve his chances for re-election in 2012.

Keep in mind that the in June 2011 the Federal Reserve (i.e., the Fed) had already completed Quantitative Easing (QE) 1 and 2, and the Fed was in no position to implement QE3. QE is nothing but gimmickry. It boils down to this. Our central bank, the Fed, prints money in one office and borrows it in another office. It's analogous to a person who has no money but has two checking accounts writing a check from one empty account to the other empty account so he can pay his bills with the bogus money in the second account. In the real world, we call it check kiting, and it's illegal. In the fantasy world that Washington has become, it's not just legal. It's regarded as good economic policy.

Releasing oil from the SPR was a dangerous substitute for QE3, and it didn't work. QE is based on fatally flawed economic thinking, and so was the SPR release. I'm tempted to say that releasing oil from the SPR proved once and for all that President Obama has lost his bearings, but I won't because you can't lose something you never

---

[54] http://articles.latimes.com/2011/jun/23/business/la-fiw-oil-20110623

had. The economy is in a very precarious position, and President Obama is flailing around like a drowning person trying to delay the inevitable.

President Obama's decision to release oil from the SPR made matters worse because the market always wins in the end. Oil will reach the price where supply and demand are in equilibrium. Nothing a president does can prevent it from happening. The same is true for real estate prices. Eventually, supply and demand will drive home prices to equilibrium, and government interventions to shore up real estate prices do nothing but postpone the agony at a huge cost to taxpayers.

President Obama had the opportunity at the beginning of his presidency to do something substantive, but he squandered it on giveaways to people and organizations that supported his candidacy in 2008—unions in particular. He must have believed that the economy would recover on its own and that throwing our money away on things that were not stimulative would have no material effects. His lavish giveaways wasted more than $2 trillion; the economy didn't recover enough because our money was misused; and now President Obama has very few options left. His much heralded stimulus/jobs proposal in September 2011 was just as foolhardy as his other forays into government largess as a substitute for sound economic policy.

The problem boils down to this. Congress can't or won't cut spending enough and/or raise taxes enough to make a noticeable difference in our long-term financial outlook; global economic growth remains sluggish; and several European countries led by Greece face insolvency. According to recent reports, the United States has just a few years left before we will face financial catastrophe[55] as well. After 3 years in office, President Obama has done nothing to improve our situation. The next president will have no choice but to tackle the real issues. If he or she fails to do it, we are in serious trouble.

---

[55] http://www.globalresearch.ca/index.php?context=va&aid=10860

The clock is ticking, and President Obama continues to ignore serious solutions preferring instead to use sleight-of-hand. That's exactly what releasing oil from the SPR was. It was similar to the "shovel-ready projects" that Obama promised in 2008 which in 2011 he freely admitted[56] never existed. We can't trust him to do the right thing because he has no idea what the right thing is. I could even say that in his liberal progressive fantasy world there is no such thing as the right thing.

Missteps at This Crucial Time Will Lead to Changes We Don't Want

Shenanigans in Washington are leading us into a perfect financial storm that could result in a worldwide economic meltdown and bring about conditions that could arouse popular global demand for a new world order. Iranian President Mahmoud Ahmadinejad is calling for one already, and he has found receptive audiences in the Shanghai Cooperation Organization[57] (SCO) and the Association of Southeast Asian Nations[58] (ASEAN). Those organizations represent the economic powerhouses of Asia including India, China, and Russia.

First, Iran called for replacing the dollar as the global reserve currency. That comes as no surprise since Iran considers the US to be the Great Satan. When the Fed initiated quantitative easing, China joined the chorus. That's not a surprise either. As I said before, China holds about a trillion dollars of US debt, and QE is little more than a program designed to print dollars and drive up inflation. I don't blame China for their concern. They were correct to point out that QE will drive down the value of their US bonds. The Chinese have a vested interest in our monetary policies. They should speak up and so should we.

---

[56] http://voices.kansascity.com/entries/obama-admits-there-were-no-shovel-ready-projects/

[57] http://www.cfr.org/international-peace-and-security/shanghai-cooperation-organization/p10883

[58] http://www.aseansec.org/

Right now, the Fed fears deflation more than inflation, so QE may make sense from the US perspective, but from China's point of view, it's a terrible deal. Inflating dollars means devaluing the dollar so that we pay off our debts with cheaper dollars. The losers are people and countries holding US debt. In the long-term, devaluing the dollar isn't the solution. In fact, it's contributing to global political and economic unrest.

For instance, QE and other efforts to devalue the dollar prompted talks in Europe about replacing the dollar as the global reserve currency. That's a big deal. It means that the tide is turning rapidly, and the dollar's days as the global reserve currency are numbered. Unfortunately, most people in the US have no idea what devaluing the dollar means. When the dollar is no longer the global reserve currency, the effect on the US economy will be breathtaking. Commodity prices will skyrocket and inflation in the US will soar.

Take a few minutes and watch the two SnyderTalk video commentaries below. Just go to YouTube and search for the titles. They will help you to understand the situation:

- What are commodities, and what do commodity prices tell us?
- The U.S. dollar is under siege and for good reasons.

The simple fact that the dollar is the global reserve currency has insulated us from the full effects of inflation so far. QE and the unwillingness of Congress and presidents from both parties to deal with our debt and deficit problems virtually guarantee that the day of the dollar IS OVER. It will take strong leadership to save the dollar—leadership that is willing to consider both spending cuts and tax increases.

As I said, this is a very big deal, and it foreshadows a changing of the guard, as it were, on the global stage. The day of the dollar as the global reserve currency will come to an end, and there will be a concomitant change in the global political structure as well. This is a major turning point in global events.

Truth is we could solve our deficit and debt problems by simply cutting spending. We generate more than enough tax revenue to pay for the things we need, but there remains in Congress enough people who want things that we don't need to win support. The need for a program is a political question, but once a program is implemented whether it is needed or not, it must be paid for. That's why I said that we must be willing to consider spending cuts and tax increases.

The 2010 midterm election was a good start at changing the political reality in Washington. The House of Representatives now has a majority that is willing to tackle tough spending issues and to rethink programs on a case-by-case basis. Hopefully the 2012 presidential election will result in major changes in the Senate and the White House. As I said, we don't have much time left. If Congress and the president don't quit playing games and solve our problems, the worst-case scenario is a realistic possibility.

I'm not trying to frighten anyone. I'm simply looking at the facts and connecting the dots. I don't have a timetable, but I will say this. If our political leaders don't get their acts together soon and start doing things that make good economic sense, it won't be long before the house of cards we've built comes tumbling down.

The Stock Market Doesn't Like What it Sees

On Thursday August 4, 2011, the Dow Jones Industrial average dropped more than 500 points, or more than 4%. That was the steepest decline in the DOW since

2008. Just a couple of days earlier, President Obama signed the debt ceiling extension bill. Most people in Washington probably thought they had calmed investor fears, but they were wrong.

Economic data suggests two things:

1. The US economy continues to be sluggish, and it's weakening.
2. Europe is a long way from having its sovereign debt issues under control.

How can this be? Didn't we spend more than $2 trillion to get the US economy moving? Didn't we engage in QE1 and QE2? And didn't the Europeans do things to stimulate their economies? Shouldn't the economies of the US and Europe be humming?

If you've thought about those questions, you're not alone. We have spent heavily in the US and Europe to get the economy going again, but it hasn't worked. President Obama has been telling us that he thinks about creating jobs all day long every day. I want to be gentle here, but that can't true. If Obama were thinking about how to create jobs and stimulate the economy

- he wouldn't be pushing green energy and trying to stifle oil, natural gas, and coal production;

- he wouldn't have ordered his regulators in agencies like the EPA to take steps to make energy consumption prohibitively expensive;

- he wouldn't have imposed Obamacare on the nation against our will at a time when the economy needed his undivided attention—not more uncertainty, which is what we got with Obamacare;

- and he wouldn't have squandered the more than $2 trillion in stimulus programs on things that benefitted his union pals at the expense of everybody else.

If you are a serious person, you have to realize that our president created this economic mess. It's not George Bush's fault. As I said earlier, it's true that the US economy started its freefall while Bush was in office, but the programs that were put in place to address the problem are all Obama's doing, and they have been a dismal failure. They were destined to fail from the get go because they never even came close to addressing the problem.

For the most part, people who have done well since the Great Recession started are Obamanistas. If you are a union member at General Motors, for example, you've done well. But in states across the nation, governors are dealing with their union problems because they don't have any choice. Their state constitutions require them to balance their budgets, and they can't do it with the union contracts that are currently in place.

In due course, union members at GM will suffer the same fate as government employee union members in Wisconsin, for instance, because their contracts have two effects on cars:

1. They drive the cost of cars higher.

2. They drive the quality of cars lower.

People who are considering buying a new car don't play by Obamanomic rules. In our president's fantasy world, he thinks that he can dictate outcomes, but car buyers are trying to get the most car they can get for their money. Despite the illusory data about GM's "success," it's just a matter of time before GM needs another handout. It might even happen before the 2012 presidential election. If I were a betting man, I would wager that our president spends more time praying that GM doesn't fall apart on his watch than he spends thinking about creating jobs.

GM is just one example of a company that has benefitted because union members tend to be Obamanistas. There are many more, and all of them have done well at our expense. Using the US treasury to pay off individuals and groups that supported Obama's candidacy in 2008 is not the way to create jobs. That's what politicians in Chicago do. It doesn't work there, and it won't work anywhere.

I'll continue with my GM example. President Obama is for green energy at the expense of fossil fuels even though green energy is little more than a pipedream at this point. There may be green energy alternatives that have the potential to produce enough energy to meet our needs at an affordable price, but they are not apparent yet. We have fossil fuels in abundance, and if we vigorously pursued their development, our energy prices would be coming down, not going up. Even more, we wouldn't be borrowing money to buy oil. Instead, we would be selling oil, coal, and natural gas to buyers around the world, producing tax revenue, and helping to solve our deficit and debt problems.

In President Obama's make-believe world, it boils down to this: "unions good", "greedy investors" bad. It should have surprised no one when Chevrolet introduced the Volt, and I hear that both people who bought a Volt like it. But ordinary people, people like you and me, wouldn't even consider buying a Volt because it's too small and too expensive.

Chevrolet produced the Volt for two reasons:

1. Obama is for green energy, and

2. GM is a union company.

The Volt doesn't make business or economic sense, but it fits perfectly with President Obama's cloudy vision. Obama used our money to bailout GM so that GM could produce cars that ordinary people don't want because they don't meet our needs. Again, don't be deceived by GM's current earnings reports. When tough times arrive, GM will fold like a cheap tent. You can count on it, and taxpayers will lose whatever stake we have in GM when it happens.

The DOW fell more than 500 points because people on Wall Street and Main Street are smarter than people on Pennsylvania Avenue—particularly the guy living in the big White House on Pennsylvania Avenue. People on Wall Street and Main Street live in the real world where facts matter and the facts tell us that Obamanomics makes no sense. Standard & Poor's understands the reality, and President Obama and his Kool-Aid drinking buddies on Pennsylvania Avenue can't change reality.

Welfare State or Freeloader Nation: They're One in the Same

We live in a freeloader nation, and things are getting worse, not better. The hang-up in the debt ceiling debate boiled down to differences of opinion about who should pay for the programs Congress has created. The freeloaders among us don't want to discuss the programs themselves and whether they are necessary. They prefer, instead, to focus their attention on the haves and have-nots. Their mantra is that the wealthy should pay their fair share.

Their fair share? Who are they trying to kid?

I've said this before, but it needs to be shouted from the housetop repeatedly. Roughly 50% of our fellow citizens pay no federal income taxes, but they are first in line for scores of government handouts. They think it's their right as citizens of the United States to live on the dole. These 2008 statistics from the National Taxpayers Union[59] need to be repeated often as well:

- The top 1% of earners paid 38.02% of federal income taxes.

- The top 5% of earners paid 58.72% of federal income taxes.

- The top 10% of earners paid 69.94% of federal income taxes.

- The top 25% of earners paid 86.34% of federal income taxes.

What's fair about that? As I said, things are getting worse, not better. It's no surprise that the freeloaders among us are up in arms. Solving our debt and deficit problems will mean that they actually have to pay something—not much mind you, but something. That's why they are willing to go to the mat and put our nation's financial future at risk, and that's why they want there to be no limit to the amount of debt that the United States takes on. Unfortunately, they have many friends in Congress, and President Obama is their champion.

Our financial problems are much worse than most people realize. For instance, consider these examples:

1. Home equity loans were created by banks to enable homeowners to borrow against the equity in their homes. As home prices skyrocketed before the housing bubble burst, masses of homeowners in the US refinanced their homes so they could take trips, buy boats, buy motorcycles, and do many other things that fit with their visions of the American Dream. When the

---

[59] http://ntu.org/tax-basics/who-pays-income-taxes.html

bubble burst, they had huge debt loads and little or no equity. In fact, many of them owed more on their homes than the houses were worth. Their desire to live as though there would be no tomorrow lies at the root of their problem. Today they are suffering the consequences, and they want Congress to bail them out.

2. Annuities and settlements are another source of cash. Many Americans have seen commercials on television where people with annuities and settlements scream, "It's my money, and I want it now." A horde of companies have been set up to pay people cash today for the annuities and settlements that could have secured their financial futures. Many of them took the bait and the money, spent the cash, and as a result, they have nothing left. Who are they turning to for help? You guessed it. Congress and their champion, Barack Obama.

3. Reverse mortgages are yet another source of cash. People who have spent themselves into financial oblivion but still have a little equity in their homes are flocking to companies that are willing to pay them cash now for the deed to their property. Some people have even promised to vacate their homes at the end of a specified amount of time in return for cash now. In other words, they will have to find a place to live in their twilight years because they've already sold their houses, and the clock is ticking. They day is coming when they will have no money and no houses. They will be wards of the government or totally dependent on their children for their sustenance.

4. Cash value in life insurance is another source of cash, and people are selling it for cash now.

These examples suggest that as a society we have adopted this philosophy: "Eat, drink, and be merry for tomorrow we die." As I said, some of our fellow citizens are spending everything they have, and there will be nothing left long BEFORE they die. Many of them will be destitute in old age and totally dependent. It's the exact opposite of the way it ought to be. Rather than passing on wealth to their children, they will leave them with mountains of unpaid bills—possibly even burial expenses. If you think I'm kidding or exaggerating, think again. It's happening right now.

The debt ceiling crisis was the tip of the iceberg, and the debt and deficit problems that we face as a nation lie just beneath the surface. But they are only part of the problem. The mountains of personal debt that people have willingly taken on virtually guarantee that their financial futures will be bleak at best. Solving that problem will require a change in the way people think, and that takes time—lots of time.

The wealthy among us who are already paying more than their fair share and who are being called upon to pay more couldn't solve our problems even if they turned over all of their assets to the feds. That hasn't stopped the freeloaders among us from demanding more "sacrifice" from them anyway. That is not the way things ought to be, but that's the way things are. To our shame, freeloader representatives in the Senate still hold a majority of the seats, and President Obama is seeking another term to champion the freeloader cause.

Is there enough time left to solve our financial problems before our system of government implodes and our nation collapses? I don't know, but I do know this. We can't keep kicking the can down the road. The longer we wait to address the problems we face as a nation, the less likely we will be able to solve them. That's why I think the 2012 presidential election will be the most important election in our nation's history, and that's why I believe the Standard & Poor's downgrade of US bonds was a good thing. It got people's attention.

Raising the Debt Ceiling Didn't Solve Our Fiscal Problems

Our nation's debt and deficit problems were not solved by raising the debt ceiling. The 2012 presidential election is the place to fight that war. I used the word "war" instead of "battle" or "fight" to describe what comes next because that's where we are politically. Why? It's because our Congress and presidents from both parties have given us an irresponsible government that is willing to spend like there will be no tomorrow, but they are unwilling to pay for what they want to buy.

This is the bottom line. We spend too much money—way too much money, but that's not all. About 50% of our fellow citizens pay no federal income taxes. They are freeloaders who take but don't give. Unfortunately, they are close to becoming the majority, and in a representative republic like ours, that's an enormous problem.

This isn't a political statement, but some will argue that it is. The Democratic Party is THE PARTY that the freeloaders among us support by a margin of roughly 99.9% to approximately 0.1%. It's the party that stands for abortion on demand without restraint, perversity of all sorts, paying people to do nothing from generation to generation, and spending without regard for the willingness or the ability to pay. Don't get me wrong. Some Republicans are just as irresponsible as Democrats, but they don't represent an overwhelming majority of the party. The real problem isn't and wasn't the debt ceiling. The real problem is the irresponsible people that we have elected and continue to elect. That makes us, the electorate, responsible for the situation we face— not Standard & Poor's.

Re-Electing Barack Obama Will Delay Solving Our Fiscal Problems Until 2016

These are the facts:

1. A wave among voters in the United States is forming.

2. Roughly 80%[60] of the people in our representative republic recognize that we have to get our fiscal house in order.

---

[60] http://www.politifact.com/truth-o-meter/statements/2011/jul/15/barack-obama/barack-obama-said-80-percent-americans-favor-both-/

3. Democrats control the Senate. The vast majority of Democratic senators think that we should always spend and tax more. It will be two more election cycles, 2012 and 2014, before the Senate reflects the mood of the country. Each election cycle, one-third of our senators face the voters. In 2010, one-third of them were up for re-election, and the conservatives won. Given the mood in our country right now and the growing realization by the majority of voters that we spend too much money already, conservatives will win in the 2012 Senate elections as well. By the end of the 2014 election cycle, the entire Senate should reflect the mood of the voters at large.

4. Members of the House of Representatives face the voters every 2 years. The House already reflects the mood of the country, and I suspect that the House will be even more conservative after the 2012 election and even more conservative than that after the 2014 election.

5. President Obama is a socialist by nature. It's who he is. He's also a Democrat. Like the Democrats in the Senate, his instincts tell him that we should always spend and tax more. In his convoluted way, he reasons that taxing and spending are the solutions to all of our problems. Even more, he thinks that we, meaning the taxpayers, should continue pouring money into union coffers so that union members will have lots of money and he can count on them to provide him with the margin of victory in 2012.

6. The debt ceiling compromise didn't solve our fiscal problems.

7. Standard & Poor's did the right thing when they downgraded US debt.

8. The 2012 election is where the war of the budget should be fought.

9. The 2012 election will be won in the middle.

10. If Barack Obama is re-elected, we can't begin to solve our fiscal problems until 2016.

Chapter 5

The "Green Energy" Scam

The fear that global warming is destroying our planet is driving President Obama's energy policies at great cost to American citizens, so the best place to begin a discussion of those policies is the theory upon which they rest. If that theory proves to be wrong, we are paying a very high price for no reason whatsoever.

In an op-ed piece for *The Washington Post* titled "On climate change, the GOP is lost in never-never land,"[61] Fred Hiatt said that he thinks Republicans live in a fantasy world and that climate change denial is just one example of their grand delusion. To be sure, some people are deluded when it comes to climate change. They're the ones who keep pushing global warming while the planet is cooling.

I'm not a Republican or a Republican Party apologist. I'm an ordinary citizen who's interested in the facts, and the facts about climate change tell a tale that Mr. Hiatt and people of his ilk can't or won't accept. They have bought into a lie so completely that they refuse to even consider evidence calling their theory into question.

The facts tell us that the climate is getting cooler.[62] For starters, consider the information in the articles below:

---

[61] http://www.washingtonpost.com/opinions/on-climate-change-the-gop-is-lost-in-never-never-land/2011/04/15/AFVLN8vD_story.html

[62] http://www.americanthinker.com/2011/04/the_climate_is_changing_alrigh.html

- Signs Of Strengthening Global Cooling[63]

- Global Cooling[64]

- Global Cooling In March[65]

- Is the Atmosphere Still Warming?[66]

One misstatement in particular stands out in Mr. Hiatt's op-ed piece. He said, "Climate science is complex, and much remains to be learned. But if you asked 1,000 scientists, 998 of them would say that climate change is real and that human activity—the burning of oil, gas and coal—is a significant contributor."

Of course, Hiatt is referring to climate change in a warmer direction because climate change per se is a given. Earth's climate has been changing since Day One. If that were not the case, then try explaining the Ice Ages and the warming periods between them.

Mr. Hiatt's assertion is troublesome because it's wrong, and dangerously so. In 2008, a group of more than 31,000 scientists[67] signed a petition dissenting from the position trumpeted by the United Nations' Intergovernmental Panel on Climate Change. More than 9,000 of them have Ph.D. degrees in fields like atmospheric science, climatology, earth science, and environmental science. That's 15 times more Ph.D.

---

[63] http://notrickszone.com/2011/01/22/signs-of-strengthening-global-cooling/

[64] http://www.philly.com/philly/blogs/weather/Global-cooling.html

[65] http://wilmington.johnlocke.org/blog/?p=5132

[66] http://wattsupwiththat.com/2011/04/13/stockwell-asks-is-the-atmosphere-still-warming/#more-37889

[67] http://www.telegraph.co.uk/news/worldnews/2053842/Scientists-sign-petition-denying-man-made-global-warming.html

scientists than are involved in the United Nations' campaign to convince the world that man-made CO_2 emissions are destroying our planet.

According to the petition, the scientific evidence leading some people to believe that human release of carbon dioxide, methane, and other greenhouse gases is causing or will cause ruinous warming of the earth's atmosphere is not convincing. One of the group's leaders, the late Professor Frederick Seitz said,

> "The United States is very close to adopting an international agreement that would ration the use of energy and of technologies that depend upon coal, oil, and natural gas and some other organic compounds …. This treaty is, in our opinion, based upon flawed ideas. Research data on climate change do not show that human use of hydrocarbons is harmful. To the contrary, there is good evidence that increased atmospheric carbon dioxide is environmentally helpful."

Seitz is a first-rate scientist who served as President of Rockefeller University and President of the U.S. National Academy of Sciences. Seitz is also a recipient of the National Medal of Science. The agreement to which he referred is the Kyoto Protocol.

Ivar Giaever, a Nobel Prize winning physicist, resigned[68] from the American Physical Society because of its position on global warming. So did University of California professor Hal Lewis. When Lewis resigned, he said that the global warming movement was a "scam" and a "pseudoscientific fraud."[69]

Seitz, Giaever, and Lewis aren't the only top scientists who have rejected global warming alarmism, but they are sufficient to prove my point. The tide is turning on

---

[68] http://www.terradaily.com/reports/Nobel_physicist_quits_US_group_over_climate_stance_999.html

[69] http://www.terradaily.com/reports/Nobel_physicist_quits_US_group_over_climate_stance_999.html

global warming mania. The only reason people like Al Gore were able to make progress pumping the issue is that world-class scientists didn't have enough spare time to fight against a movement that they believed only intellectual lightweights would embrace.

Be that as it may, if you are writing for one of the nation's leading newspapers, you should make an effort to get your facts straight. In this case, Mr. Hiatt is presenting his unsubstantiated opinions about climate change as proven scientific fact that only crackpots refuse to recognize, and he's not alone. Liberal progressive politicians and journalists do the same thing every day, and contradictory hard evidence is either foolishly ignored or willfully covered up no matter what its source.

This is a serious matter that concerns all of us because our government is in the process of imposing strict controls to reduce greenhouse gases in hopes of staving off global warming even though earth's atmosphere is cooling, and the cost to you and me is higher energy prices, higher inflation, and a lower standard of living since every product we buy has an energy cost component.

Under new leadership, the House of Representatives recently took steps to prevent the Environmental Protection Agency (EPA) from using the Clean Air Act to regulate CO_2 emissions, but President Obama made it clear that he will continue to pursue his agenda regardless of the facts. The EPA, under orders from the president, is moving ahead[70] aggressively with regulations that touch each one of us in profound ways. Obama's misguided effort to stay the course by fiat or by executive order isn't just wrong minded. It's very expensive, and it's a price that we can ill afford to pay, especially now as our economy is struggling to recover from the Great Recession.

---

[70] http://www.americanthinker.com/2011/09/epa_fundamental_transformation_through_regulation.html

The theory to which global warming alarmists cling is fatally flawed, and they are doing everything they can to prevent the truth from getting out. In SnyderTalk, I present articles frequently that contain factual information about climate change. Below are the titles of several recent examples:

- Climate change: this is the worst scientific scandal of our generation

- Climategate: the final nail in the coffin of 'Anthropogenic Global Warming'?

- ClimateGate: The Fix is In

- Scientists in Climate-Gate Scandal Hid Data

- The Real Climategate Scandal

- 'Climate-Gate' Scandal Should Be Wake-Up Call For Press, Politicians

- Temperature Monitors Report Widescale Global Cooling

- Global Cooling Is Coming—and Beware the Big Chill, Scientist Warns

- The Global Climate Change Debate—The Facts

- IPCC scientist: Global cooling headed our way for the next 30 years?

The facts presented in these articles lead to the following conclusions:

1. There are lots of climate scientists who believe we have entered a global cooling phase.

2. The number of scientists who believe global cooling has arrived is growing.

3. Frightened because factual data doesn't support their wild claims, global warming alarmists have resorted to hiding data, making up data, and doing everything in their power to keep data that challenges their theory from seeing the light of day.

To deny that our climate is cooling you have to ignore a mountain of hard data, and the facts are mounting year-by-year—facts that prove the theory relied on by global warming alarmists is wrong. For example, it was comical to watch the participants at the December 2010 UN Global Warming Summit in Cancun, Mexico dress for winter as temperatures plunged to a 100-year record low.[71] That kind of thing is happening all over the world, and it's not anecdotal data. It's a global trend that only diehard global warming alarmists refuse to accept.

There is more, much more. For instance, did you know that the number of global weather tracking stations has been reduced,[72] and disproportionately the eliminated stations are in colder regions? Even so, global warming alarmists have continued to report data showing global temperatures rising despite the fact that colder locations have been taken out of the data set, and they didn't bother to divulge that critical piece of information.

This isn't complicated. If you take cold readings out of the data set, average temperatures will rise, but it has absolutely nothing to do with actual global temperatures. If you included the temperature inside my oven in the data set, average temperatures would rise as well, but it would be a sham. Need I say more?

The climate is cooling,[73] and it's been cooling since 1998.[74] Eventually, the truth will prevail, but in the meantime, Obamanistas and other alarmists continue to retard progress at great cost to US taxpayers and energy consumers. The only people profiting

---

[71] http://theweek.com/article/index/210181/irony-alert-the-unusually-chilly-global-warming-summit

[72] http://wattsupwiththat.com/2008/03/06/weather-stations-disappearing-worldwide/

[73] http://www.climatecooling.org/

[74] http://www.telegraph.co.uk/comment/personal-view/3624242/There-IS-a-problem-with-global-warming...-it-stopped-in-1998.html

from the global warming hysteria are global warming alarmists who are selling a pig in a poke. President Obama is firmly in the global warming hysteria camp. In fact, he is their champion.

Climate Complexities

Warming cycles have built-in governors that limit their longevity. Slow moving deep-sea currents carry ocean water from the equatorial region to the polar regions and back. Those currents moderate the climates at both poles and at the equator. Warmer ocean water associated with warm cycles melts pack ice at the poles, and ocean water becomes less salty. That's critical because the saltier the water, the faster the current, and vice versa.

As pack ice melts, ocean water becomes less salty and deep-sea currents slow down. That causes temperatures at the poles to fall and glaciers to advance. That's what I mean by built-in governors, and it's a natural cycle. Man didn't cause it to happen, and man can't do anything to prevent it from happening.

Many variables influence the earth's climate. For example, about 95 percent of the greenhouse effect we hear so much about is caused by ordinary water vapor. That's H_2O, not CO_2, and there's nothing wrong with it. Also, methane is about 26 times more powerful as a greenhouse gas than CO_2, and the warming atmosphere and oceans cause the release of huge quantities of methane that's locked up in ocean floor sediment and polar permafrost as methane hydrate.

Cutting CO_2 emissions won't influence the release of methane one iota. It won't cause volcanoes to stop spewing out particulate matter, CO_2, and sulfur dioxide—that's SO_2, another greenhouse gas. Did you know that there are roughly 22 volcanoes erupting at any given moment? That means there are at least 22 volcanoes spewing out greenhouse gases at this very moment, and it's been like that for thousands and thousands of years.

That's why it makes no sense to look only at man-made CO_2 emissions. No responsible scientist would do that. Other variables are far more important. For instance, sun spots, solar winds, variations in the solar magnetic field, and solar irradiation have enormous effects on our climate. Cutting CO_2 emissions certainly won't alter the sun's activity, and it won't change earth's orbit either.

This may be news to some people, but earth's orbit cycles between circular and elliptical. Obviously, when earth is in a more elliptical orbit and it's at the far end of the orbit, the climate is colder. This is the bottom line, the average person doesn't have any idea how complicated our climate is. Al Gore has received a lot of attention because his message is so incredibly simple. It's simple beyond belief, and it's just plain wrong— some would say "stupid."

I wrote a novel focusing on the climate change scam titled Stand! My goal is to educate people about what's really happening in an entertaining way. Stand! is available at Amazon. The title of the book has a hyperlink. Click on it, and it will take you to the Amazon webpage. In the upper right corner of the webpage, you'll see a box containing the words "Buy now with 1-click." Below that you'll see Available on your PC. You'll need this for downloading eBooks from Kindle, and the software is free. Next, directly under "Buy now with 1-click," you see "Deliver to." The drop down will enable you to select "Kindle for PC" and download Stand! directly into your computer. You can also download it for use with Kindle devices, iPads, Sony Readers, and a host of other tablet devices. You'll need to have an account with Amazon. If you don't have one already, I recommend it strongly.

Al Gore: Lunatic, Fraud, or Bullshit Artist?

August 2011[75]—There Al Gore was in all of his radiant glory in Aspen, Colorado surrounded by the so-called "intellectual elite" sounding forth on important issues of the day. His wisdom, or more correctly his lack of wisdom, was on display for all to see. Al Gore has a penchant for connecting dots. Problem is the dots he connects may or may not be related. They may not even be dots. Most of Al Gore's so-called "facts" are figments of his imagination.

As you would expect, Al Gore had something to say about global warming, and he was experiencing a fit of rage. It's best if you hear it straight from the horse's mouth. I don't want anyone to accuse me of misquoting a former vice president much less a winner of the Nobel Peace Prize. Visit "http://soundcloud.com/realaspen/audio-recording-on-monday" to hear Al Gore rant.

Al Gore's upset because the tide is turning in the world and thinking people are beginning to question the pseudo science upon which he has built a reputation and a fortune. He's been peddling hokey about global warming since he left office and now people are casting aspersions his way. It's no wonder that Al Gore is on the defensive.

Others are feeling the heat as well. For instance, so-called "professionals" at East Anglia University[76] have been exposed for manipulating data and doing their utmost to prevent the facts about climate change from getting out, and to this day, Michael Mann, creator of the infamous "hockey stick" chart purporting to show that manmade carbon

---

[75] http://www.realaspen.com/article/767/Speaking-in-Aspen-Colorado-Al-Gore-calls-bullshit-on-global-warming-naysayers

[76] http://www.telegraph.co.uk/earth/copenhagen-climate-change-confe/6678469/Climategate-University-of-East-Anglia-U-turn-in-climate-change-row.html

emissions are destroying the planet, is being protected by the University of Virginia, my university.

Virginia's attorney general, Ken Cuccinelli,[77] thinks Mann may have used public funds to support his research that he contends was little more than a ploy to perpetuate a hoax at public expense. Eventually, the facts about those emails will get out, just like the facts about East Anglia University got out, and UVA may have some explaining to do.

If there is nothing culpatory in those emails, the logic for refusing to comply with the attorney general's subpoena[78] is not apparent. In fact, you can make a strong argument that UVA is complicit in the matter because its leaders are standing in the way of justice, but that's another story. As I said, the facts will eventually be told, and then we'll know the truth.

Al Gore's crime isn't selling snake oil to a gullible public. He's contributing to the imposition higher energy costs on the public at large—costs that they can ill afford to pay—and threatening our way of life. His views may be losing their luster with the masses, but they are the foundation upon which liberal progressives like Barack Obama have built their plan to remake America in ways that we don't understand. Despite what he says, science is on the side of those who question Al Gore's theory. So why is President Obama championing "green energy" at the expense of fossil fuels?

---

[77] http://bearingdrift.com/2011/05/25/judge-orders-uva-to-hand-over-michael-manns-emails/

[78] http://www.thegwpf.org/the-climate-record/2520-climategate-virginia-assembly-upholds-right-to-subpoena-michael-mann.html

Obama's "Green Energy" Fetish

President Obama has a "green energy" fetish, and its effect on food prices shouldn't be minimized because food and energy inflation are taking a big bite out of US consumers' paychecks, and they are contributing to world hunger. Consider ethanol, for example. For the 2011-2012 marketing year,[79] the US has mandated that 13 billion gallons of biofuels will be produced—almost all of it coming from corn. At a minimum, 4.65 billion bushels of US corn will be diverted to ethanol production, thus depriving a hungry world of that precious source of nutrients and driving up the price of corn for those who can afford to buy it.

The chart below shows the price of corn in dollars per metric ton between 2000 and 2011. As you can see, the price of corn is skyrocketing, and there is no end in sight.

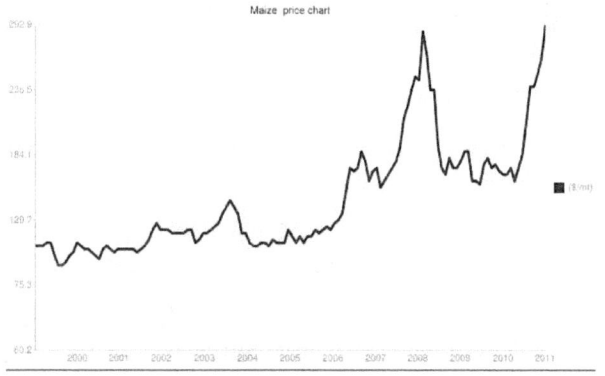

10-year commodity price chart for Maize (Corn)

Source: Compiled by mongabay.com using figures from World Bank Commodity Price Data.[80]

---

[79] http://www.blackseagrain.net/about-ukragroconsult/news-bsg/most-of-the-focus-on-2011-us-planted-acreage-centers-on-corn-acreage

[80] http://www.mongabay.com/images/commodities/charts/maize.html

The Facts about Ethanol

Few people know the facts about ethanol:[81]

- "Ethanol is listed as a known human carcinogen by the International Agency for Research on Cancer.

- The cost of Reformulated Gasoline with ethanol will increase 3-6 cents per gallon compared to RFG with MTBE.

- Spills of pure ethanol or gasoline containing ethanol from leaking storage tanks can create a benzene plume up to 150% larger than a spill from a non-ethanol fuel.

- Ethanol cannot be shipped by pipeline because of its high affinity for water, posing significant distribution costs and hurdles for gasoline blenders.

- According to a study by Cornell University, for every gallon of ethanol produced 1.4 gallons of energy is consumed in the process, compared to 0.15 gallons used in the manufacture of gasoline.

- It takes 1.5 gallons of ethanol (E-85) to drive as many miles as one gallon of gasoline.

- Every gallon of ethanol removes 53 cents from the Federal Highway Trust Fund because of a special tax break for producers.

- Ethanol increases the vapor pressure of gasoline by 1 psi resulting in higher evaporative emissions of Volatile Organic Compounds, while tailpipe emissions of Acetaldehyde increase 150%.

- Ethanol permeates the hoses and lines of automobile fuel systems resulting in a 50% increase in VOC emissions for pre-1995 cars.

- Ethanol dissolves oxide scale from the walls of pipes and tanks, subjecting the systems to internal corrosion, which leads to leaks."

---

[81] http://www.calgasoline.com/facttopten.htm

Ethanol production reduces tax revenue from the sale of gasoline; it drives up the price of gasoline at the pump and contributes to inflation; it damages vehicles and increases repair costs; and it robs the world of a food staple. The only thing ethanol has going for it is a president with a "green energy" fetish. If the decision to blend ethanol with gas had been made based on the merits of the case, there would no ethanol blend fuel on the US market today.

Driving Up Energy Prices by Hook or by Crook

While running for the highest office in the land, in a televised interview[82] candidate Barack Obama promised that under his administration "electricity rates will skyrocket." As president, he has delivered on that promise. In the interview, candidate Obama was referring specifically to driving up coal prices, but his actions as president have proven beyond any reasonable doubt that the coal industry was not his only intended victim. His administration has targeted our country's entire energy sector with the exception of "green energy" firms which happen to be his favorites and made the United States more dependent on foreign oil.

The president got off to a rousing start in 2009:[83]

- "February 4, 2009—he withdrew areas offered for 77 oil and gas leases in Utah that could cost American taxpayers millions in lost lease bids, production royalties, new jobs and the energy needed to offset rising imports of oil and natural gas. According to a Uintah County commissioner, this prevented the creation of approximately 3,000 jobs.

---

[82] http://www.youtube.com/watch?v=HlTxGHn4sH4&feature=player_embedded

[83] http://naturalresources.house.gov/Issues/Issue/?IssueID=15410

- February 10, 2009—he delayed for six months the development of the new 5-year leasing program for offshore drilling that would have created new jobs, produced more American-made energy, and made us less dependent on foreign oil.

- February 25, 2009—he delayed the new round of oil shale research, demonstration, and development (RD&D) leases that would help advance American technology and create high-tech jobs in Colorado, Wyoming and Utah. According to a study prepared for The National Energy Technology Laboratory, over 350,000 jobs would be created by the development of our oil shale resources.

- February 26, 2009—he introduced a budget that contains page after page of taxes on American energy totaling more than $31 billion and included a cap-and-trade national energy tax that could cost the average American family over $3,100 a year.

- April 17, 2009—his Environmental Protection Agency listed carbon dioxide as a hazardous pollutant, opening the door for the regulation of all CO2 emissions under the Clean Air Act.

- April 27, 2009—his Environmental Protection Agency ordered the cancellation of a permit for a Navajo Nation power plant that Navajo leadership called the most important development project the tribe has ever undertaken. The plant was expected to create 400 permanent jobs and generate $50 million per year in revenue.

- June 29, 2009—his Interior Department established new solar reserve areas under the premise of prioritizing solar development, but the actual result was the closing of all but two percent of federal lands from renewable energy development. This was done without public comment. The Department left open only 670,000 acres of the nearly 30 million acres of land with solar potential.

- July 20, 2009—he blocked new uranium mining for two years on one million acres of land in Arizona.

- • October 8, 2009—he issued a final report on the Utah oil and natural gas leases, offering only 17 of the 77 leases. In November, the Institute for Energy Research found that the administration has leased less acreage than any other on record.

- October 20, 2009—he announced a new round of oil shale RD&D Leases that included job-destroying variable terms, royalty rates, and lease sizes."

Obama pressed ahead aggressively with his crusade to destroy the American energy industry in 2010:[84]

- "January 6, 2010—he implemented numerous new hurdles to the leasing and development of new oil and natural gas on onshore federal lands.

- January 26, 2010—his Minerals Management Service announced it would delay the Virginia offshore lease sale scheduled for November 2011.

- January 28, 2010—he announced the results of the most recent round of oil shale RD&D leases, which resulted in an 85% reduction in industry interest under the terms proposed by the Department.

- February 1, 2010—he released the FY 2011 budget proposal that included nearly $40 billion in direct tax and fee increases on American energy production, which would increase gasoline and energy prices for American families and businesses.

- February 17, 2010—his Department of Energy notified Congress that it would reprogram $115 million Congress appropriated to continue the Yucca Mountain licensing process, and instead use it to terminate the only national repository for spent nuclear fuel under current law.

---

[84] http://naturalresources.house.gov/Issues/Issue/?IssueID=15410

- March 3, 2010—his Department of Energy filed a motion to permanently abandon Yucca Mountain – the nation's repository for high-level spent nuclear fuel under current law – jeopardizing the future of nuclear energy.

- March 12, 2010—he withdrew 61 oil and natural gas leases in Montana as part of a lawsuit settlement over climate change.

- March 31, 2010—ignoring statutory law, his Bureau Of Land Management agreed to settle a lawsuit out of court regarding the use of an "extraordinary circumstances" provision when using "categorical exclusions" for new oil and gas leases as defined by Section 390 in the Energy Policy Act (EPAct) of 2005.

- March 31, 2010—he announced a new offshore drilling plan that closed large portions of our offshore areas from future energy production.

- May 6, 2010—he issued a moratorium on all new drilling in the Gulf of Mexico, creating further economic devastation and costing up to 12,000 jobs according to the administration's own estimates.

- May 17, 2010—his Bureau of Land Management finalized rules, first announced by Secretary Salazar on January 6, 2010, to establish more government hurdles to onshore oil and natural gas production on federal lands.

- May 28, 2010—he officially lifted the moratorium on shallow water drilling – yet continued to slow-walk the issuing of permits, creating a de facto moratorium.

- June 15, 2010—in an Oval Office address on the Deepwater Horizon oil spill, President Obama continued to push for implementation of a job destroying cap-and-trade national energy tax.

- July 12, 2010—he issued a new moratorium on deepwater drilling after the first moratorium was struck down in federal court.

- July 19, 2010—his President's Ocean Policy Taskforce issued final recommendations on implementing a Federally-controlled system of ocean zoning that could lock up huge areas of the ocean to energy development.

- October 12, 2010—he lifted the deepwater drilling moratorium – yet continued to keep the de facto moratorium in place by slow-walking the issuing of permits.

- October 14, 2010—his Bureau of Ocean Energy Management issued an interim safety rule for the Gulf of Mexico, which stated that OPEC could offset a decrease in Gulf of Mexico deepwater production as a result of the administration's de facto moratorium.

- November 18, 2010—an Interior Department presentation showed that they plan to postpone new lease sales in the Gulf of Mexico until 2012.

- November 30, 2010—his Interior Department announced it would consider proposals to regulate hydraulic fracturing on public lands – a technique currently regulated by states that is responsible for tremendous growth in natural gas production.

- December 1, 2010—he effectively reinstated the ban on offshore drilling, placing the entire Pacific coast, the entire Atlantic coast, the Eastern Gulf and parts of Alaska off limits to future energy production until 2017 at the earliest.

- December 23, 2010—his interior Department announced a new "Wild Lands" Secretarial Order that could place hundreds of millions of acres of public lands off-limits to American energy production."

As energy prices have climbed steadily in 2011, President Obama has maintained his commitment to "green energy" at the expense of oil, natural gas, and coal.[85] Demonstrating that he is politically tone-deaf where energy is concerned, he has ignored the effects of his policies on the nation even though members of Congress from both parties have come out against many of his initiatives. Obama's zeal to drive up the price of energy is breathtaking:

---

[85] http://naturalresources.house.gov/Issues/Issue/?IssueID=15410

- "January 14, 2011—he retroactively pulled a permit for a West Virginia coal mine, costing 250 American jobs.

- February 2, 2011—Federal Judge finds the Interior Department in contempt of court for continuing to slow-walk Gulf of Mexico drilling permits.

- February 14, 2011—he released the FY 2012 budget proposal that includes over $60 billion in direct tax and fee increases on American energy production, which would raise gasoline and energy costs for all Americans.

- February 15, 2011—he announced further delays to U.S. oil shale production by deciding to re-review the current rules for commercial oil shale leasing.

- February 17, 2011—a federal judge ordered the Obama administration to act on five pending deepwater permits within 30 days.

- February 28, 2011—he issued a token deepwater permit, over four months after the moratorium was officially lifted. But continued to slow-walk permits, keeping the de facto moratorium in place and leaving thousands of Americans out of work.

- March 4, 2011—rather than end the de facto moratorium, the Obama administration filed an appeal to a federal court ruling that ordered them to act on stalled deepwater permits."

The United States Should be Exporting its Surplus Energy

The United States has been blessed with enough energy resources to run our factories, light our cities and homes, and feed our people and the people of the world, but we have not developed them the way we should have. Instead, we have been cowed by liberal progressives who would rather sunbathe in luxury without unsightly drilling platforms on the horizon. Most of those platforms are beyond the horizon, so it's our way of life that they really loathe.

In 2008, the US imported almost 13,000,000 barrels of oil per day, or about 57% of our total oil consumption. Although our energy needs have been increasing rapidly, the US didn't build a new refinery between 1998 and 2008, even then over the strong objections of liberal progressives. In 2008 alone, the US spent almost $500,000,000,000 on imported oil. That's half a trillion dollars that we didn't need to spend. Our dependence on foreign oil is putting our economy and our national security at risk.

Saying that the US is rich in energy resources is an understatement. At today's consumption levels, we have enough coal to meet our needs for the next 500 years.[86] We have 22,450,000,000 barrels of proven oil reserves,[87] and we are finding new oil reserves all the time. The US has 250 trillion cubic feet of proven natural gas reserves.[88] We are finding new gas reserves daily, and we are discovering new ways to tap into hard-to-get gas deposits. Putting that in perspective, the US has more energy in natural gas than the entire Middle East has in oil.[89] It's disgraceful that we're putting our economic security and our national security at risk to import strategic resources that we have in abundance.

T. Boone Pickens, one of the world's leading oil and gas men and an energy investor, has launched a campaign to reduce our dependence on foreign oil by developing our natural gas reserves. His plan is called the Pickens Plan. Pickens deserves our support, but we need to do more. We must develop our coal, oil, and natural gas reserves. We also need to develop wind energy, solar energy, and hydrogen energy. There is absolutely no excuse for the United States to import oil and gas from another nation.

---

[86] http://www.eia.gov/energyexplained/index.cfm?page=coal_reserves

[87] http://www.nationmaster.com/graph/ene_oil_res-energy-oil-reserves

[88] http://reason.com/blog/2011/01/20/what-energy-crisis-natural-gas

[89] http://www.youtube.com/watch?v=8ac3H21jjco

We have already spent more than $2,000,000,000,000[90] on a vast array of stimulus programs since President Obama took office. That's several times more than will be needed to fully develop all of our energy resources. We have squandered our wealth to reward individuals and groups that supported candidate Obama in 2008 while our critical economic and security needs have gotten scant attention. We can't afford four more years of President Obama.

"Green energy" may satisfy our energy needs one day, but this much is certain. Today "green energy" is little more than a way for President Obama to dole out federal dollars to his favorite firms at the expense of coal, oil, and natural gas producers. The science and technology do not exist in so-called "green energy" areas to meet even a smidgen of our energy needs. Even so, there is no reason to believe that President Obama won't continue doing what he has been doing as long as he has the keys to the Oval Office, and there is no one to blame for our high and rising energy prices except President Obama.

Solyndra's Gone, but How Many More Solyndras Are There?

Solyndra is a solar energy company. It's also a favorite of President Obama, or at least it used to be one of his favorites. The president praised[91] the company for helping to meet our energy needs and for creating new high-tech jobs. He even made a video[92] about the company to convince voters that stimulus spending was a good use of taxpayer money.[93] That was before the company failed and put the United States

---

[90] http://www.nwherald.com/mobile/article.xml/articles/2011/09/07/05125339/index.xml

[91] http://www.youtube.com/watch?v=KYiJ-_K9NCo

[92] http://www.youtube.com/watch?v=0lVKTmLMV_M&feature=player_embedded

[93] http://www.weeklystandard.com/blogs/white-house-video-touted-solyndra-stimulus-success-story_593071.html

government on the hook for $535 million[94] in loan guarantees—money that taxpayers will have to pay because of our president's "green energy" fetish.

The House of Representatives is investigating the Obama administration's involvement in the Solyndra deal. According to House Energy Committee Chairman Fred Upton (R-Michigan), "We have learned from our investigation that White House officials monitored Solyndra's application and communicated with [Department of Energy] and Office of Management and Budget officials during the course of their review."[95] There seems to be little doubt that the White House pressured The Office of Management and Budget (OMB) and ignored Energy Department concerns to get the Solyndra deal approved.[96]

The FBI raided Solyndra's offices[97] to obtain information about possible misuse of federal funds, and you can be sure of this. House and FBI investigators will uncover the facts. Even before all the facts were gathered, the Obama administration resorted to its old mainstay—in case of an emergency BLAME BUSH.[98] Of course, it won't work, but when you have no defense for your actions, you do the best that you can. We know that emails connecting the Obama administration to Solyndra reach into the White House—specifically Vice President Biden's office.[99] A connection to the Oval Office may or may not emerge, but only an idiot would believe that President Obama wasn't intimately involved in the Solyndra deal.

---

[94] http://www.weeklystandard.com/blogs/uh-oh-house-investigating-bankrupt-green-jobs-company-obama-admin-ties_592114.html

[95] http://www.weeklystandard.com/blogs/uh-oh-house-investigating-bankrupt-green-jobs-company-obama-admin-ties_592114.html

[96] http://www.weeklystandard.com/blogs/white-house-pressured-omb-ignored-energy-dept-concerns-approve-solyndra-loan_593524.html

[97] http://www.csmonitor.com/Business/Latest-News-Wires/2011/0909/FBI-Solyndra-raid-misuse-of-federal-loans

[98] http://www.weeklystandard.com/blogs/new-white-house-strategy-solyndra-debacle-blame-bush_593566.html

[99] http://finance.townhall.com/columnists/bobbeauprez/2011/09/14/emails_link_solyndra_to_biden_office

The facts paint an ugly portrait of Obama administration officials using their influence with funding agencies and the OMB to get the Solyndra loan guarantee approved despite obvious problems that were identified by people with enough expertise to evaluate the company. That should come as no surprise since Solyndra investors, board members, and executives were all big Obama donors.[100] Solyndra is an example of politics as usual—Chicago style. The Obama administration even let $385 million in taxpayer support for Solyndra take a back seat to funds from new investors.[101] That's not just foolish. It's stupid, but we'll still have to pay.

I don't want to focus too much attention on Solyndra because, as they say, "Where there is smoke, there is fire." You can bet that there are many more Solyndras out there waiting to be discovered[102]—firms like LightSquared, for instance. According to *Pajamas Media*, LightSquared's "owner happens to be a big Democratic Party donor. And in the pursuit of giving preference to a specific company, the White House undercut a legendary four-star general (William Shelton) and potentially undermined U.S. national security. Adding fuel to the explosive story: at one time President Obama was a personal investor, with $50,000 of his own money."[103]

According to a report in *The Daily Beast*,[104] the White House pressured Shelton to alter his testimony about a $14 billion internet project that Shelton believed would threaten the Pentagon's Global Positioning System. That system is crucial to our

---

[100] http://www.weeklystandard.com/blogs/solyndra-obama-administration-had-mutually-beneficial-relationship_592078.html

[101] http://www.bloomberg.com/news/2011-09-03/taxpayers-rank-behind-solyndra-s-investors-under-obama-refinancing-deal.html

[102] http://www.foxnews.com/politics/2011/09/15/despite-stimulus-funding-solyndra-and-4-other-companies-have-hit-rock-bottom/

[103] http://pjmedia.com/blog/lightsquared-another-solyndra/?singlepage=true

[104] http://www.thedailybeast.com/articles/2011/09/15/lightsquared-did-white-house-pressure-general-shelton-to-help-donor.html

national security. If these stories turn out to be true or even partly true and there are more like them, then President Obama may be guilty of more than just poor leadership. We may find that he has manipulated our government for personal and/or political gain. Given Obama's circle of close friends in Chicago, that wouldn't be a great surprise. All the jokes about the Obama administration being a form of "gangster government" may be true.

Be that as it may, as of September 2011 according to *The Blaze*,[105] the $38.6 billion "green energy" program that President Obama said would create 65,000 jobs had proven to be a dismal failure. By that time, more than $19 billion in awards had been granted, and only 3,545 jobs had been created. The return on our "investment" was poor—very poor. The cost per job created turned out to be more than $535,000. Solyndra's failure resulted in 1,100 jobs lost. When you subtract those jobs, the cost per job created is just under $800,000. It's no wonder that President Obama has a difficult time understanding that our nation's economic security is at stake.

Even under the best of circumstances and working with people of integrity, high-tech new ventures are high-risk propositions. Most new ventures fail as they should, and that's one important reason why we should not gamble that unproven "green energy" projects will meet our nation's energy needs. A very small percentage of those new ventures will turn out to be good investments—one day in the sweet by-and-by, but most of them won't. In the meantime, our cars need gas and our children need food.

This is the bottom line. Obama's "green energy" program is an abysmal failure.[106] You know for a fact that a Democratic president has problems when *The Washington Post* points that out.

---

[105] http://www.theblaze.com/stories/govt-awards-nearly-19-billion-in-loan-guarantees-to-create-3545-green-jobs/

[106] http://www.weeklystandard.com/blogs/wapo-obamas-green-energy-loan-program-bust_593586.html

It's foolish to put America's economic and national security at risk because a president, any president, has a fetish for a utopian energy environment—one in which energy is available in abundance to everyone at a very low price with absolutely no risk to the environment. We don't live in that kind of world. We live in the real world where tradeoffs have to be made. The person who holds the highest office in the land shouldn't gamble with our money and our security to obtain campaign contributions and/or personal wealth. If that's not a criminal offense, it should be.

President Obama has made his choices, and they're bad ones. He's thrown coal, oil, and natural gas under the bus—resources that we have in abundance, and he's cast his lot with unproven and risky alternatives most of which will prove to be dismal failures just like Solyndra. That's not leadership. It's idiocy, but evidence suggests that he may have done much more than that. He may have traded things we hold dear, our economic and national security, for personal and/or political gain.

President Obama's home state, Illinois, has a long and sordid history of gangsterism and of sending politicians to prison for wrongdoing while in office. Half of Illinois governors since the 1970s have gone to prison, or they are heading in that direction.[107] I suppose it's possible that the president is trying to establish a similar tradition in our nation's capital. As I said before, Barack Obama makes Richard Nixon look like a choirboy. Nixon resigned from office to avoid a trial and a potential prison term. It's too early to speculate about Obama's destiny.

---

[107] http://www.chicagonow.com/jane-of-all-trades/2011/06/half-of-illinois-governors-have-gone-to-jail-since-the-1970s/

Chapter 6

Barack Obama and Radical Islam

Radical Islam is a growing problem throughout the world.[108] In Europe,[109] it's a burgeoning issue that politicians have been unwilling to address properly because of the growing influence of Muslims in Europe,[110] but it's a critical problem in the United States[111] too—especially in our nation's prisons.[112] That's an undeniable fact, and US politicians have been reluctant to deal with it. The mood in the US is so anti-anti-Islam that the political class runs for the exit whenever Islam is raised as an issue. Not so with Representative Peter King (R-New York). He endured death threats[113] and criticism from liberal progressives that he is an Islamophobe because he held hearings in the House of Representatives to investigate the growing Islamist threat we face as a nation. The same people who screamed bloody murder because Representative King took his job in the House seriously will be the first in line to raise a ruckus if/when a homegrown terrorist nutjob, maybe an ex-convict who is out on parole, attacks innocent men, women, and children in this country.

---

[108] http://www.onenewsnow.com/Journal/stories.aspx?id=73891

[109] http://www.foreignaffairs.com/articles/60829/robert-s-leiken/europes-angry-muslims

[110] http://www.youtube.com/watch?v=CSWLLc6uikE

[111] http://www.radicalislam.org/threat/homegrown-threat/us-mosques

[112] http://www.foxnews.com/politics/2011/06/15/law-enforcement-officials-claim-radical-islam-infiltrating-us-prisons/

[113] http://theconservativetreehouse.com/2011/03/08/rep-peter-king-islamic-death-threats-media-attacks-cair-propaganda-and-gop-wishy-washy-full-roundup/

I'm reminded of a scene in the movie *Ghost Writer* starring Ewan McGregor and Pierce Brosnan. Brosnan plays a former British Prime Minister who is being charged with crimes against humanity in the International Criminal Court (ICC) in Geneva, Switzerland for trying to prevent terrorist attacks in Great Britain. Toward the end of the movie, Brosnan tells his ghost writer (Ewan McGregor) that if he had it to do all over again, he would have 2 lines for people boarding planes out of England. The first line would lead to planes carrying passengers whose terrorist affiliations and connections were not investigated, and the second line would lead to planes carrying passengers who had been cleared. He says, in effect, "You know which planes the chronic complainers would board. Every one of them would choose a plane that we cleared."

The movie may be fiction, but it touches on a very real problem. World leaders who take their jobs seriously and act to deal with the growing Islamist militancy problem that's spreading across the globe like a putrid infection are at risk of being charged with crimes against humanity or worse in the ICC. For example, President George W. Bush was forced to cancel a trip to Geneva[114] in February 2011 to avoid being charged with crimes against humanity for the role he played as President of the United States in creating the federal prison in Guantanamo Bay (GITMO) where the US holds captured terrorists. Despite assurances[115] that he would close GITMO immediately if he was elected president, Barack Obama has failed to follow through with that promise because it made no sense when he made it, and it still makes no sense. As I have said before, President Obama talks too much, and much of what he says is totally off-the-wall if not dishonest.

The real crime, one that doesn't get enough attention, is that leaders around the world who do their jobs end up putting their lives and their reputations at risk for doing exactly what they should do. There is no shortage of loud-mouthed buffoons in the world, and radical Islamists are doing their best to engage the fools among us in a

---

[114] http://www.globalresearch.ca/index.php?context=va&aid=23111

[115] http://www.youtube.com/watch?v=8USRg3h4AdE

global public relations campaign to criminalize actions that prevent rabid killers from carrying out deadly attacks with impunity. Their ploy is working, and the ICC is their venue of choice to intimidate people who pose potential threats to their quest for global jihad and global domination by Islamist militants.

We owe a debt of gratitude to President Bush and to Representative King for protecting our safety on their watch. Keep these things in mind because the 2012 election is about which group will hold the reins of power in this country. Will we elect serious people or people like Barney Frank, Nancy Pelosi, and Barack Obama? They have done more damage in and to this country than you can imagine, and President Obama's foolishness is on display all over the world. In the Middle East, he's creating a nightmare that we will have to suffer through, and it's just beginning for us. The Israelis are already feeling the heat because of our president's misguided policies. That's the subject of the next chapter.

Radical Islam has Infiltrated Countries around the World

An article in a June 2011 issue of *The Weekly Standard* titled "From Somalia to Nigeria: Jihad"[116] is correct as far as it goes, but it stops far short of revealing the extent to which radical Islamists have infiltrated countries around the world. From Somalia to Nigeria is across the heart of Africa from the Arabian Sea to the South Atlantic, but jihadists have a major presence in every North African country too, from Morocco[117] to Egypt.[118] Their presence in the Middle East is obvious as well from Saudi Arabia[119] to Lebanon[120] and Syria,[121] but it doesn't stop there. They have

---

[116] http://www.weeklystandard.com/blogs/somalia-nigeria-jihad_574838.html

[117] http://www.csmonitor.com/2003/1215/p07s01-woaf.html

[118] http://inthearena.blogs.cnn.com/2011/02/01/tonight-radical-muslim-clerics-take-on-egypt/

[119] http://www.radicalislam.org/content/saudi-arabias-coming-revolution

[120] http://www.israelnationalnews.com/News/News.aspx/116694#.Tr2XmUMUq7s

created strongholds in Iran,[122] Afghanistan,[123] and the Indian subcontinent.[124] Their reach extends from India[125] to the Philippines[126] and Indonesia[127] and into the heart of Asia[128] from China[129] to Russia.[130]

Jihadists are alive and well across Europe[131] too, but their presence doesn't stop there either. They have footholds in most South American[132] countries including Venezuela,[133] Bolivia,[134] and Brazil.[135] Like tentacles from a thriving cancer, jihadists have extended their reach from Mexico[136] to the United States[137] to Canada.[138]

---

[121] http://www.jihadwatch.org/2004/05/radical-islam-spreading-in-syria.html

[122] http://www.radicalislam.org/threat/iranian-threat/radical-islam-and-iran

[123] http://www.paklinks.com/gs/pakistan-affairs/210449-a-brief-history-of-radical-islam-in-afghanistan-and-its-origins.html

[124] http://www.tomorrowsworld.org/special_report/the-indian-sub-continent-on-the-edge-of-chaos

[125] http://www.sify.com/news/radical-islams-war-with-india-news-columns-jegvsvggjce.html

[126] http://www.danielpipes.org/comments/30297

[127] http://seaf.stanford.edu/news/radical_vs_moderate_islam__in_indonesia_a_war_rages_20031204/

[128] http://www.atimes.com/atimes/Front_Page/GH23Aa01.html

[129] http://www.reuters.com/article/2008/07/28/us-china-politics-islam-idUSPEK15873220080728

[130] http://www.hurriyetdailynews.com/n.php?n=russias-tatarstan-warns-of-threat-from-radical-islam-2011-05-30

[131] http://www.foreignaffairs.com/articles/60829/robert-s-leiken/europes-angry-muslims

[132] http://www.jamestown.org/programs/gta/single/?tx_ttnews%5Btt_news%5D=623&tx_ttnews%5BbackPid%5D=180&no_cache=1

[133] http://www.adl.org/main_International_Affairs/venezuela_anti_semitism_report.htm?Multi_page_sections=sHeading_2

[134] http://www.thegatewaypundit.com/2009/06/blog-post/

[135] http://news.gather.com/viewArticle.action?articleId=281474979205398

[136] http://mypetjawa.mu.nu/archives/180456.php

Saying that radical Islam is a problem that the entire world has to confront is a gross understatement. It's not about politics. It's about eradicating a festering sore before it turns into gangrene and threatens our very existence. World leaders have been slow to act, and the infection is spreading like wildfire.

The time for playing political football and focusing on idiosyncratic differences is over. It's time to deal with radical Islam before jihadists deal with us. We don't need a president who bows and scrapes before Islamic despots in hopes of currying favor. We need a president who is willing to lead the leaders of the world in a global mission before it's too late. We didn't declare war on jihadists. They declared war on us, and they are deadly serious. We should be too.

The Islamist Threat is Too Serious to Elect Dilettantes and Ignoramuses

Prominent attorney and Harvard law professor Alan Dershowitz wrote an interesting article titled "Norway Needs a Single Standard Against Terrorism."[139] In it, he pointed out that after a terrorist attack on Norway, Norway's Ambassador to Israel said that Hamas' terrorist activity against Israel is more justified than terrorist attacks against Norway. His logic was simple, naïve, and asinine. "We Norwegians," he said, "consider the occupation to be the cause of the terror against Israel."

First things first, the land in question isn't "occupied." It's "disputed land." There is a huge difference. People in Norway need to get it straight and so do people in other nations around the world.

---

[137] http://www.washingtontimes.com/news/2010/aug/5/radical-islams-conquest-of-america/?page=all

[138] http://pjmedia.com/blog/canada-must-boost-anti-islamist-efforts-at-home/

[139] http://www.hudson-ny.org/2310/terrorism-norway-israel

Second, Islamofascists have made it clear that they have set their sights on the entire world. They publicly admit that they want a one world caliphate where Sharia law applies. Of course, they don't really mean that. They don't want the rule of any law. They are nothing more than subversive butchers, murderers, and thieves — Islamist anarchists as it were. They are a threat to everyone, Muslims included. They don't even like each other. They do whatever they want whenever they want, but most of the time they don't publicly promote their barbarous atrocities as their favorite method for gaining global supremacy. Even people in Norway would object to that, so they couch their argument in terms that are likely to win enthusiastic support from ignorant dilettantes. Judging by the Norwegian ambassador's comments, they have won him over.

Third, the terrorist attack on Norway wasn't carried out by a radical Islamist. It was perpetrated by Anders Breivik, a man who was reported by media hacks to be a Christian. Reading his manifesto[140] proves that's not so, but the anti-Christian point of view sells well in a world where it's okay to attack Jews and Christians, but not Muslims.

I suspect that we are witnessing the beginning of a global backlash against radical Islamists in the wake of government unwillingness to address the problem in a serious manner. In a nutshell, I'm saying that I don't think Breivik was a lone wolf. Neither do I believe that the anti-Islamists are connected in a formal sense, not yet anyway, but that day may come.

When governments fail to do their jobs, people take matters into their own hands. I'm not defending Breivik, and I'm not excusing his brutal, unprovoked attack on innocent victims, many of which were children. I'm simply stating a fact, and I'll repeat it again to make sure that my message is clear. If people who are charged with

---

[140] http://www.scribd.com/doc/60739170/2083-a-European-Declaration-of-Independence

the responsibility to secure our nations won't do their jobs, vigilante justice will result. It's a dangerous consequence of government failure.

You are not an Islamophobe if You Think Radical Islam is a Threat

In the United States today among the self-professed "enlightened ones," the prevailing view is that people who see a Muslim threat to global peace and security are Islamophobes. I'm one of those people and you probably are too, but I'm not afraid of Islam—the religion. I am concerned about the space cadets, airheads, dimwits, and useful idiots who have to ignore mountains of evidence to conclude that radical Islam isn't a threat to the world as we know it.

Israel in particular is under threat because Islamists in Egypt, Saudi Arabia, Jordan, Syria, Lebanon, Iraq, and Iran have committed their lives and everything they possess to bring about her destruction. That's perfectly clear in the Hamas Charter and in the Palestinian Charter.[141] If you look at the map on the next page, you'll see that Israel is completely surrounded by her enemies, and President Obama thinks that Islamists can be placated by giving them pieces of the already tiny country. Anyone who buys that line of reasoning is not just drinking the Kool-Aid. He or she suffers from psychotic delusions.[142]

Iran is the head of the enemy group, and her leaders mean business. Ignoring Iran's threats/warnings and her attempts to influence every country in the Middle East is ludicrous because she has the will and the resources to launch a coordinated attack.

---

[141] http://www.snydertalk.com/?page_id=2760

[142] http://emedicine.medscape.com/article/292991-overview

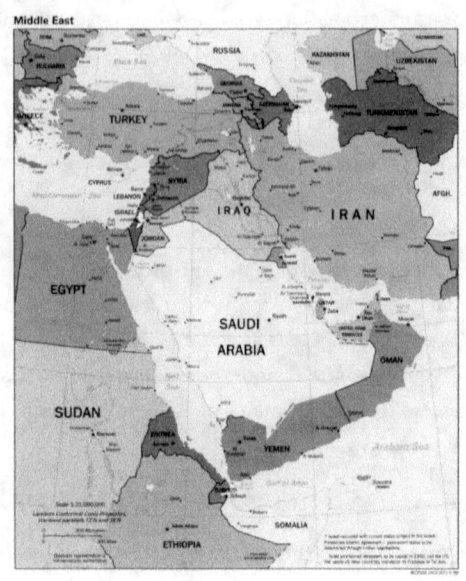

The Arab Spring has Created Lots of Uncertainty

Revolutions are tricky things, and revolution is spreading like a wildfire throughout the Middle East. Egypt is a primary concern because the Egyptian government has already fallen, and Egypt remains the most powerful Arab nation in the Middle East militarily. No one can say for sure who will lead Egypt following the ouster of Hosni Mubarak. Even so, Amr Moussa, a 74-year-old former foreign minister for Mubarak and past head of the Arab League, has a leg up on the competition in the race to become the next Egyptian president. An article in *Jewish World Review* about Moussa by Dan Ephron titled "Egypt's Rising Power Player"[143] is worth reading.

---

[143] http://www.jewishworldreview.com/0711/moussa.php3

Moussa has a commanding lead over his leading competitor, Mohamed ElBaradei, the former Director General of the International Atomic Energy Agency (IAEA). A poll conducted in June 2011 by Ipsos shows that Moussa leads the list of presidential wannabes in Egypt with 25% support; ElBaradei is second with just 5% support; and the rest of the field is for all practical purposes out of the running. A similar poll taken in March showed that Moussa had 40% support, so the race for the Egyptian presidency is by no means settled. With roughly 57% of Egyptian voters still undecided, anything could happen, but Moussa is courting the Islamist vote and he's likely to get it. ElBaradei remains a heavy favorite among the protesters who toppled Mubarak's regime.

More than anything else, Moussa has this going for him. He is well known for his "anti-Israel diatribes." According to Ephron's article, Moussa said, "I will tell you two things: No. 1, that the treaty, we're not going to abrogate it. And No. 2 … We want to rebuild the country, and rebuilding the country by necessity [means] not to follow an adventurous policy." But Moussa also said, "The peace process has become a dirty word, because we discovered it was just [an Israeli] trick to continue talking and make the cameras flash … but there's no substance. We shall not engage in such a thing anymore. Never."

Moussa may be just another run-of-the-mill politician like President Obama pandering to various voting blocks to win their support, but we don't know for sure. This much we do know. Moussa is and has been one of Egypt's most relentless critics of Israel. We know this, too. More than half of the Egyptian people favor annulling the peace treaty with Israel.[144] A pandering politician eventually succumbs to the pressure and gives likely voters what he thinks they want. Does that spell doom for the peace treaty between Israel and Egypt? It's impossible to say for sure at this time, but don't rule it out.

---

[144] http://www.jpost.com/MiddleEast/Article.aspx?id=217883

According to Ephron, one Western diplomat said that "the source of his (Moussa's) popularity is almost entirely derived from his image as an Arab nationalist who's very critical of Israel." To me, that sounds like he's moving rapidly toward the Islamofascist camp in Egypt. Will he complete the journey? Again, it's impossible to know for sure right now, but we need to keep a close eye on developments. If Egypt goes Islamist, for all practical purposes, Israel will have no friends in the region, and with Obama in the White House, she has no friend in the Oval Office.

The day may arrive soon when Israel has no friends in the world. At that point, the Israelis will have no choice but to rely on themselves. That won't be enough to insure Israel's survival, so eventually the nation Israel will have to turn to Yahweh. He's their only hope, and the day is coming when they will realize it. This is how Yahweh explained it to Zechariah:

"In that day I will make the clans of Judah like a firepot among pieces of wood and a flaming torch among sheaves, so they will consume on the right hand and on the left all the surrounding peoples, while the inhabitants of Jerusalem again dwell on their own sites in Jerusalem. Yahweh also will save the tents of Judah first, so that the glory of the house of David and the glory of the inhabitants of Jerusalem will not be magnified above Judah. In that day Yahweh will defend the inhabitants of Jerusalem, and the one who is feeble among them in that day will be like David, and the house of David will be like God, like the angel of Yahweh before them. And in that day I will set about to destroy all the nations that come against Jerusalem. I will pour out on the house of David and on the inhabitants of Jerusalem, the Spirit of grace and of supplication, so that they will look on Me whom they have pierced; and they will mourn for Him, as one mourns for an only son, and they will weep bitterly over Him like the bitter weeping over a firstborn." (Zechariah 12: 6-10)

But Egypt isn't the only country in the Middle East experiencing turmoil associated with the Arab Spring. Yemen, Bahrain, Libya, Syria, and Jordan to name just a few countries are dealing with Islamist threats that were under control before revolution broke out in Tunisia. The United States has a failed history[145] of dealing with the Islamist threat, and under Barack Obama, things have gotten worse—not better. Part of Obama's problem on the global stage is a problem that US citizens have come to know all too well. He thinks he knows everything even when he knows nothing, and he won't budge from his position even after facts proving that he is wrong are readily available. Too much is at stake to re-elect President Obama.

In chapter 1, I mentioned a friend who wanted the United States to elect a black president. His logic was simple. He said, "Presidents can't do too much damage." Look at the evidence. Do you agree with his assessment? If not, you shouldn't even consider voting for President Obama. In fact, you should do everything you can to help elect someone else.

---

[145] http://pjmedia.com/blog/the-u-s-government%E2%80%99s-failed-history-of-muslim-outreach-since-911/

Chapter 7

You Can't be Pro-Obama and Pro-Israel

Barack Obama has failed to achieve the bipartisan results that he promised to seek while running for office. In fact, he has created a chasm between the political left and right in this country that is wider than it has ever been.

The president's tendency to shove his ideas down people's throats regardless of their merits, the biting partisan rhetoric that he aims at political opponents, the condescending way that he talks down to legislators with more experience and better ideas than his, the "this is not about me" mantra that he uses repeatedly to insult anyone who dares to challenge his ideas, and his incessant posturing are huge parts of his problem. The president has even managed to alienate the far left in his own party. Some say that's because he's too centrist, but anyone who calls Barack Obama a centrist[146] has to ignore his long and sordid history of leftist positions on a broad range of issues and his radical far left friends and advisors.

The president has been able to unite one group, though—the people of New York's 9th congressional district. There they call him The Uniter[147] because he was able to accomplish something that no one had been able to do since before the Great Depression. In a heavily Jewish and Democratic district, his treatment of Israel brought the voters together to elect a Republican. The message was loud and clear. They had

---

[146] http://townhall.com/columnists/thomassowell/2008/10/27/obama_and_the_left/page/full/

[147] http://www.youtube.com/watch?feature=player_embedded&v=G4_L_uUdfBY

had enough, and they weren't going to take any more. We need to send Obama the same message in 2012.

Barack Obama is no Friend of Israel

Since the day he took office, President Obama has been anti-Israel. He has taken advantage of every opportunity to snub Israeli Prime Minister Benyamin Netanyahu; he has created false hope among so-called "Palestinians"; and he has fomented problems in the Middle East that Israel is being forced to suffer through. This isn't speculation. It's fact.

"Dithering" is an apt word for describing the president's policies regarding Israel. I've mentioned dithering before. In a nutshell, it means that the president doesn't have an Israel policy. He makes it up as he goes along, and nothing is certain except that he has created a colossal mess in the entire Middle East.

For example, what were the president's policies regarding freedom-seeking Arabs who wanted changes in their political systems during the Arab Spring? Hosni Mubarak, Egypt's president, had to go and so did Muammar Gaddafi, Libya's president, but what about Syrian President Bashar al-Assad? President Obama wasn't sure about him. As of September 2011, the death toll in Syria was more than 2700[148] and rising, but the Obama administration did little or nothing to quell the senseless violence perpetrated against the Syrian people by Mr. Assad.

President Obama's Israel policy is just as incoherent. At one point, Obama summoned Israeli Prime Minister Binyamin Netanyahu to the White House for a

---

[148] http://in.reuters.com/article/2011/09/19/idINIndia-59426920110919

tongue-lashing and a well-publicized, deliberate snub.[149] After some political upheaval at home because of his Israel policies and rapidly changing events in the Middle East, Mr. Obama wasn't so sure about the Israel situation any longer, but he did hear something about 1967 borders that sounded like a winner politically. Palestinian President Mahmoud Abbas said Israel's 1967 border should be her permanent border, and so did Syrian President Bashar al-Assad.

Obama dithered in that direction immediately, gave another speech,[150] and created another ruckus.[151] Problem is Israel's 1967 "border" and all the "borders" before it weren't borders. They were armistice lines. Israel has been fighting wars for survival since 1948, and each war has been defensive. At the end of each conflict, new armistice lines were created. The 1967 armistice line and those before it are not relevant in any way except as propaganda tools.

It was no coincidence that Obama delivered his speech[152] just before Prime Minister Netanyahu was scheduled to arrive in Washington for an official visit. The outcry[153] from people in this country who love Israel was strong and swift so the president backpedaled as best he could, but he also started pressuring Israel[154] to agree to negotiate on the 1967 lines. Reports indicated that the pressure was intense.[155] In

---

[149] http://www.telegraph.co.uk/news/worldnews/barackobama/7521220/Obama-snubbed-Netanyahu-for-dinner-with-Michelle-and-the-girls-Israelis-claim.html

[150] http://www.msnbc.msn.com/id/43091459/ns/world_news-mideast_n_africa/t/obama-tells-israel-borders-key-peace/#.Tr2dcUMUq7s

[151] http://www.nytimes.com/2011/05/20/world/middleeast/20speech.html?_r=2

[152] http://wvgazette.com/News/201105201424

[153] http://abcnews.go.com/Politics/obama-speech-backlash-call-reinstate-1967-mideast-borders/story?id=13639200

[154] http://www.washingtontimes.com/news/2011/jun/10/white-house-seeks-israeli-agreement-to-negotiate-o/

[155] http://www.commentarymagazine.com/2011/06/12/obama%E2%80%99s-not-done-hammering-israel-on-1967-lines/

short order, the European Union[156] came out in favor of Obama's '1967 borders' speech saying in effect that Israel should return to the 1967 border.

Netanyahu rejected[157] the proposal, as he should have, but this question stands out in my mind. Why would our president solicit and then take the advice of Israel's enemies and make a major policy proposal concerning Israel's future without consulting with Israel first? That makes absolutely no sense unless you realize that Barack Obama is no friend of Israel, and it leads to this conclusion. You can't be pro-Obama and pro-Israel.

Trying to force Israel to accept indefensible borders is preposterous. It's a step in the process of eradicating Israel completely. If you took away all of the land that Israel has gained in wars for survival, Israel would have no land. That's exactly what Palestinian leaders want. In their world, Israel doesn't exist.[158] Israel doesn't even appear on their maps[159] and the logo for the Permanent Observer Mission of Palestine to the United Nations that's in use today shows the entire land of Israel as "Palestinian" territory:

[156] http://www.haaretz.com/print-edition/news/eu-pushing-peace-plan-based-on-obama-s-1967-borders-speech-1.367512

[157] http://thehill.com/blogs/blog-briefing-room/news/162189-after-obama-speech-israel-rejects-return-to-1967-borders

[158] http://www.israelnationalnews.com/News/News.aspx/143611#.Tr2ejkMUq7s

[159] http://www.terrorism-info.org.il/malam_multimedia/english/eng_n/pdf/as_nm_e.pdf

For symbolic reasons, Yasser Arafat wore his headdress in the shape of the tiny country that he hoped to destroy. He died trying to destroy Israel, but he didn't succeed. In the picture below, Arafat was preparing for a photo shoot. He wanted his headdress to be just right for photographers:

Jerusalem in the Bible

Jerusalem is mentioned more than 700 times in the Old Testament and 144 times in the New Testament. Jerusalem isn't mentioned by name even once in the Koran. So why all the fuss among Arab Muslims about Jerusalem? It's because Jerusalem is holy to Yahweh.

Below are several passages from the Bible that deal with Jerusalem. Read them and see for yourself what Yahweh has said about Jerusalem:

- Psalm 122: 6—Pray for the peace of Jerusalem: may they prosper who love you.

- Psalm 137: 5-7—If I forget you, O Jerusalem, may my right hand forget her skill. May my tongue cling to the roof of my mouth if I do not remember you, if I do not exalt Jerusalem above my chief joy. Remember, O Yahweh, against the sons of Edom the day of Jerusalem, who said, "Raze it, raze it to its very foundation."

- Psalm 147: 2—Yahweh builds up Jerusalem; He gathers the outcasts of Israel.

- Isaiah 62:6-7— On your walls, O Jerusalem, I have appointed watchmen; all day and all night they will never keep silent. You who remind Yahweh, take no rest for yourselves; and give Him no rest until He establishes and makes Jerusalem a praise in the earth.

- Zechariah 8:22—'So many peoples and mighty nations will come to seek Yahweh Sabaoth in Jerusalem and to entreat the favor of Yahweh.'

- Zechariah 9: 9—Rejoice greatly, O daughter of Zion! Shout in triumph, O daughter of Jerusalem! Behold, your king is coming to you; He is just and endowed with salvation, humble, and mounted on a donkey, even on a colt, the foal of a donkey.

- Zechariah 12: 2-14—"Behold, I am going to make Jerusalem a cup that causes reeling to all the peoples around; and when the siege is against Jerusalem, it will also be against Judah. It will come about in that day that I will make Jerusalem a heavy stone for all the peoples; all who lift it will be severely injured. And all the nations of the earth will be gathered against it. In that day," declares Yahweh, "I will strike every horse with bewilderment and his rider with madness. But I will watch over the house of Judah, while I strike every horse of the peoples with blindness. Then the clans of Judah will say in their hearts, 'A strong support for us are the inhabitants of Jerusalem through Yahweh Sabaoth, their God.'"

"In that day I will make the clans of Judah like a firepot among pieces of wood and a flaming torch among sheaves, so they will consume on the right hand and on the left all the surrounding peoples, while the inhabitants of Jerusalem again dwell on their own sites in Jerusalem. Yahweh also will save the tents of Judah first, so that the glory of the house of David and the glory of the inhabitants of Jerusalem will not be magnified above Judah. In that day Yahweh will defend the inhabitants of Jerusalem, and the one who is feeble among them in that day will be like David, and the house of David will be like God, like the angel of Yahweh before them. And in that day I will set about to destroy all the nations that come against Jerusalem."

"I will pour out on the house of David and on the inhabitants of Jerusalem, the Spirit of grace and of supplication, so that they will look on Me whom they have pierced; and they will mourn for Him, as one mourns for an only son, and they will weep bitterly over Him like the bitter weeping over a firstborn. In that day there will be great mourning in Jerusalem, like the mourning of Hadadrimmon in the plain of Megiddo. The land will mourn, every family by itself; the family of the house of David by itself and their wives by themselves; the family of the house of Nathan by itself and their wives by themselves; the family of the house of Levi by itself and their wives by themselves; the family of the Shimeites by itself and their wives by themselves; all the families that remain, every family by itself and their wives by themselves."

- Zechariah 14: 1-21 — "Behold, a day is coming for Yahweh when the spoil taken from you will be divided among you. For I will gather all the nations against Jerusalem to battle, and the city will be captured, the houses plundered, the women ravished and half of the city exiled, but the rest of the people will not be cut off from the city. Then Yahweh will go forth and fight against those nations, as when He fights on a day of battle. In that day His feet will stand on the Mount of Olives, which is in front of Jerusalem on the east; and the Mount of Olives will be split in its middle from east to west by a very large valley, so that half of the mountain will move toward the north and the other half toward the south. You will flee by the valley of My mountains, for the valley of the mountains will reach to Azel; yes, you will flee just as you fled before the earthquake in the days of Uzziah king of Judah. Then Yahweh, my God, will come, and all the holy ones with Him!"

"In that day there will be no light; the luminaries will dwindle. For it will be a unique day which is known to Yahweh, neither day nor night, but it will come about that at evening time there will be light."

"And in that day living waters will flow out of Jerusalem, half of them toward the eastern sea and the other half toward the western sea; it will be in summer as well as in winter."

"And Yahweh will be king over all the earth; in that day Yahweh will be the only one, and His name the only one."

"All the land will be changed into a plain from Geba to Rimmon south of Jerusalem; but Jerusalem will rise and remain on its site from Benjamin's Gate as far as the place of the First Gate to the Corner Gate, and from the Tower of Hananel to the king's wine presses. People will live in it, and there will no longer be a curse, for Jerusalem will dwell in security."

"Now this will be the plague with which Yahweh will strike all the peoples who have gone to war against Jerusalem; their flesh will rot while they stand on their feet, and their eyes will rot in their sockets, and their tongue will rot in their mouth. It will come about in that day that a great panic from Yahweh will fall on them; and they will seize one another's hand, and the hand of one will be lifted against the hand of another. Judah also will fight at Jerusalem; and the wealth of all the surrounding nations will be gathered, gold and silver and garments in great abundance. So also like this plague will be the plague on the horse, the mule, the camel, the donkey and all the cattle that will be in those camps."

"Then it will come about that any who are left of all the nations that went against Jerusalem will go up from year to year to worship the King, Yahweh Sabaoth, and to celebrate the Feast of Booths. And it will be that whichever of the families of the earth does not go up to Jerusalem to worship the King, Yahweh Sabaoth, there will be no rain on them. If the family of Egypt does not go up or enter, then no rain will fall on them; it will be the plague with which Yahweh smites the nations who do not go up to celebrate the Feast of Booths. This will be the punishment of Egypt, and the punishment of all the nations who do not go up to celebrate the Feast of Booths."

"In that day there will be inscribed on the bells of the horses, "HOLY TO YAHWEH." And the cooking pots in Yahweh's house will be like the bowls before the altar. Every cooking pot in Jerusalem and in Judah will be holy to

111

Yahweh Sabaoth; and all who sacrifice will come and take of them and boil in them. And there will no longer be a Canaanite in the house of Yahweh Sabaoth in that day."

According to the Bible, Yahweh will make Jerusalem a cup that causes reeling to all the peoples around. He will make Jerusalem a heavy stone for all the peoples; all who lift it will be severely injured. He will gather all the nations against Jerusalem for battle. Then Yahweh will go forth and fight against those nations. That's what Yahweh said will happen, and that's what is happening.

According to Yahweh, the Promised Land Belongs to Israel

If you are a believer, this should be your central question: What does Yahweh say about Israel's borders? Nothing else matters.

- "Now lift up your eyes and look from the place where you are, northward and southward and eastward and westward; for all the land which you see, I will give it to you and to your descendants forever. I will make your descendants as the dust of the earth, so that if anyone can number the dust of the earth, then your descendants can also be numbered. Arise, walk about the land through its length and breadth; for I will give it to you." (Genesis 13: 14-17)

- "To your descendants I have given this land, from the river of Egypt (the Nile River) as far as the great river Euphrates; the land of the Kenite and the Kenizzite and the Kadmonite and the Hittite and the Perizzite and the Rephaim and the Amorite and the Canaanite and the Girgashite and the Jebusite." (Genesis 15: 18-21)

112

- "For My part, this is My covenant with you: you will become the father of many nations. And you are no longer to be called Abram; your name is to be Abraham, for I am making you father of many nations, and your issue will be kings. And I shall maintain my covenant between Myself and you, and your descendants after you, generation after generation, as a covenant in perpetuity, to be your God and the God of your descendants after you. And to you and to your descendants after you, I shall give the country where you are now immigrants, the entire land of Canaan, to own in perpetuity. And I will be their God." (Genesis 17: 4-8)

- "As regards your wife…Sarah….I shall bless her and moreover give you a son by her. I shall bless her and she will become nations: kings of peoples will issue from her….Yes, your wife Sarah will bear you a son whom you must name Isaac. And I shall maintain My covenant with him, a covenant in perpetuity, to be his God and the God of his descendants after him. For Ishmael too I grant you your request. I hereby bless him and will make him fruitful and exceedingly numerous. He will be the father of twelve princes, and I shall make him into a great nation. But my covenant I shall maintain with Isaac, whom Sarah will bear you…." (Genesis 17: 15-16 and 19-21)

- "Do not go down to Egypt; stay in the land of which I shall tell you. Sojourn in this land and I will be with you and bless you, for to you and to your descendants I will give all these lands, and I will establish the oath which I swore to your father Abraham. I will multiply your descendants as the stars of heaven, and will give your descendants all these lands; and by your descendants all the nations of the earth shall be blessed; because Abraham obeyed Me and kept My charge, My commandments, My statutes and My Laws." (Genesis 26: 2-5)

- "I am Yahweh, the God of your father Abraham and the God of Isaac; the land on which you lie, I will give to you and your descendants. Your

113

descendants shall also be like the dust of the earth, and you shall spread out to the west and to the east and to the north and to the south; and in you and in your descendants shall all the families of the earth be blessed. Behold, I am with you and will keep you wherever you go, and will bring you back to this land; for I will not leave you until I have done what I have promised." (Genesis 28: 13-15)

- "You shall no longer be called Jacob, but Israel shall be your name....I am God Almighty (El Shaddai); be fruitful and multiply; a nation and a company of nations shall come from you, and kings shall come forth from you. The land which I gave to Abraham and Isaac, I will give it to you, and I will give the land to your descendants after you." (Genesis 35: 10-12)

- "I am Yahweh, and I will bring you out from under the burdens of the Egyptians, and I will deliver you from their bondage. I will also redeem you with an outstretched arm and with great judgments. Then I will take you for My people, and I will be your God; and you shall know that I am Yahweh your God, who brought you out from under the burdens of the Egyptians. I will bring you to the land which I swore to give to Abraham, Isaac, and Jacob, and I will give it to you for a permanent possession; I am Yahweh." (Exodus 6: 6-8)

- "Behold, I am going to send an Angel before you to guard you along the way and to bring you into the place which I have prepared. Be on your guard before Him and obey His Voice; do not be rebellious toward Him, for He will not pardon your transgression, since My Name is in Him. But if you will truly obey His Voice and do all that I say, then I will be an enemy to your enemies and an adversary to your adversaries. For My Angel will go before you and bring you in to the land of the Amorites, the Hittites, the Perizzites, and the Canaanites, the Hivites and the Jebusites; and I will completely destroy them. You shall not worship their gods, nor serve them, nor do

114

according to their deeds; but you shall utterly overthrow them and break their sacred pillars in pieces. But you shall serve Yahweh your God, and He will bless your bread and your water; and I will remove sickness from your midst." (Exodus 23: 20-25)

- "I will send My terror ahead of you, and throw into confusion all the people among whom you come, and I will make all your enemies turn their backs to you. I will send hornets ahead of you that they may drive out the Hivites, the Canaanites, and the Hittites before you. I will not drive them out before you in a single year, that the land may not become desolate and the beasts of the field become too numerous for you. I will drive them out before you little by little, until you become fruitful and take possession of the land. I will fix your boundary from the Red Sea to the sea of the Philistines (i.e., the Mediterranean Sea), and from the wilderness to the River Euphrates; for I will deliver the inhabitants of the land into your hand, and you will drive them out before you." (Exodus 23: 27-31)

Saying that Israel's border matters to Yahweh is an understatement. If that were not so, He wouldn't have said so much about the border, and He didn't leave any wiggle room about its precise location.

Do you think President Obama or any other human being has the right to ignore Yahweh's plan and make up one of his own? Hardly. The question about Israel's border is a test of sorts. It's about faith. Do we have faith in Yahweh? The answer is either "yes" or "no." There is no "I'm not sure" option. Where we come down on this issue tells more about our faith than anything we say. I can't emphasize the importance of this issue enough.

Yahweh's promises concerning the Promised Land[160] are not starting points from which negotiations are supposed to begin. He made those promises to Abraham, Isaac, and Jacob, and they are fixed for all eternity. To nonbelievers, those promises are just words; to most Arabs, they are of no consequence; but to Yahweh and His people they are sacrosanct.

Below is a picture of Israel's border that Yahweh delineated:

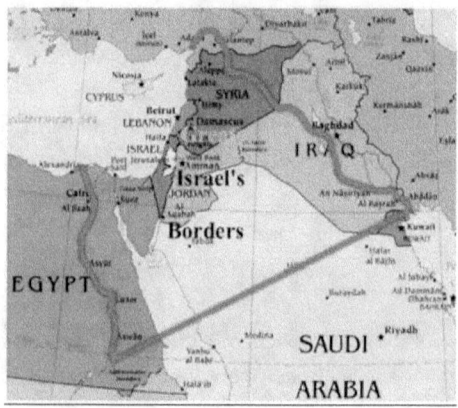

Yahweh's Promises Will be Fulfilled No Matter What People Try to Do

The Oslo Accords[161] grew out of the Madrid Conference[162] in October 1991. They were completed in August 1993 and signed on September 13, 1993. The two-state solution we hear so much about today was mapped out in the Oslo Accords, and since

[160] http://www.snydertalk.com/?page_id=2490

[161] http://en.wikipedia.org/wiki/Oslo_Accords

[162] http://en.wikipedia.org/wiki/Madrid_Conference_of_1991

the Oslo Accords were signed, movement toward the creation of a Palestinian state inside Israel has been the primary pursuit of the Quartet—the United States, Europe, Russia, and the UN. The United States was the pivotal player in the formulation of the Oslo Accords.

George Bush, the father, was president of the United States when the Madrid Conference convened in 1991. At that time, he was considered a shoo-in for re-election. The very day that the Madrid Conference convened, The Perfect Strom[163] hit the Eastern Atlantic Seaboard of the United States doing great damage to the Bush compound[164] on Walker's Point in Kennebunkport, Maine. A best-selling novel by Sebastian Junger titled *The Perfect Storm* and a movie by the same title starring George Clooney captured the imaginations of millions and preserved the legacy of that storm for future generations. In November 1992, George Bush, the father, was defeated by an obscure Arkansas governor named Bill Clinton.

Are these just coincidences, or is there more to the story? Read on.

- Yahweh made a promise to Abraham: "Now Yahweh said to Abram, 'Go forth from your country, and from your relatives and from your father's house, to the land which I will show you; and I will make you a great nation, and I will bless you, and make your name great; and so you shall be a blessing; and *I will bless those who bless you, and the one who curses you I will curse.* And in you all the families of the earth will be blessed." (Genesis 12: 1-3)

- Yahweh made a promise to Isaac: "Do not go down to Egypt; stay in the land of which I shall tell you. Sojourn in this land and I will be with you and bless

---

[163] http://www.ncdc.noaa.gov/oa/satellite/satelliteseye/cyclones/pfctstorm91/pfctstorm.html

[164] http://en.wikipedia.org/wiki/Bush_compound

you, for to you and to your descendants I will give all these lands, and I will establish the oath which I swore to your father Abraham. I will multiply your descendants as the stars of heaven, *and will give your descendants all these lands,* and by your descendants all the nations of the earth shall be blessed; because Abraham obeyed Me and kept My charge, My commandments, My statutes and My Laws." (Genesis 26: 2-5)

- Yahweh made a promise to Jacob: "I am Yahweh, the God of your father Abraham and the God of Isaac; *the land on which you lie, I will give it to you and to your descendants.* Your descendants will also be like the dust of the earth, and you will spread out to the west and to the east and to the north and to the south; and in you and in your descendants shall all the families of the earth be blessed. Behold, I am with you and will keep you wherever you go, and will bring you back to this land; for I will not leave you until I have done what I have promised you." (Genesis 28: 13-15)

Is there a connection between Yahweh's promises regarding the Promised Land and the events surrounding the Oslo Accords? Does Yahweh really intervene to bless those who bless Israel and curse those who cruse Israel? Read on.

- When Moses led the Children of Israel out of Egypt, they were a large group. There were at least 2 or 3 million people and there may have been as many as 6 million people traveling with Moses. Rulers of the nations through which the Children of Israel walked along with their herds and flocks were terrified. A group that large could easily consume virtually all the vegetation in the land and drink most of the available fresh water. Those rulers did not know that Yahweh miraculously provided food and water for His children.

- As they marched toward the land of Moab, which is in Jordan today, they fought with and defeated the King of Arad, the King of the Amorites, and the

King of Bashan. When they reached Moab, the Moabite King, Balak, sent for Balaam because he was well-known as a man who possessed the ability to bless or to curse. Balak wanted Balaam to curse Israel and to destroy them. Yahweh appeared to Balaam in Person and said, "You shall not curse the people, for they are blessed." (Numbers 22: 12)

- Balak had offered to pay Balaam a large sum of money if he would curse the Children of Israel, so he tried his best to get permission from Yahweh to curse them. Eventually, Yahweh appeared to Balaam in Person with a sword in His hand ready to strike if Balaam did not change his mind. (Numbers 22: 23) Balaam went on to bless the Children of Israel much to the disappointment of Balak, but Yahweh never forgave Balaam for his evil intent and for his deceit and lustful desire to destroy God's chosen people for money. (Jude 11)

Yahweh is and always has been Israel's Protector. He blesses those who bless Israel, and He curses those who curse Israel. If you are not a believer, this is gobbledygook to you, but if you are a believer, you see Yahweh's hand in events that are shaping our destiny and the destiny of Israel.

President Obama is pressuring Israel to move ahead with a peace deal that will divide the Promised Land, threaten the sanctity of Jerusalem, the holiest city in the world to Yahweh, and threaten Israel's security. We call Israel the Promised Land for one reason. Yahweh promised it to Abraham and his descendants through Isaac and Jacob. Are there consequences for interfering with Yahweh's fulfillment of those promises? Some say "yes" and others say "no," but this is not a matter of opinion. It's an empirical question that has a right or wrong answer. Judging by what the Bible says and what I see, the answer is unquestionably "yes."

The United States is once again standing in the way of Yahweh's promise to unite Israel and Judah and bring them to the Promised Land where they can live in peace. Now is the time to decide whose side you are on. If you are for Yahweh, you can't be against Israel. If you are against Israel, you can't be for Yahweh. Similarly, if you are pro-Obama, you can't be pro-Israel. It's as simple as that.

Facts about the West Bank and the Middle East Peace Process

Where Israel is concerned, the mainstream media has done a terrible job of reporting. Most of the so-called "facts" they present aren't facts, and the truth seldom sees the light of day. Below are two short videos that will help you to understand the West Bank and the Middle East peace process. Please take a few minutes to watch them. You'll be glad you did.

- Israel Palestinian Conflict: The Truth About the West Bank[165]
- Israel Palestinian Conflict: The Truth About the Peace Process[166]

The Palestinian and Hamas Charters

The Palestinian and Hamas Charters[167] reveal an ugly truth that you need to take hold of. You can access them by clicking on the hyperlink in the previous sentence, or you can read them in the Appendix at the end of this book. You need to read the documents themselves to fully appreciate what Israel is up against. If you don't realize what Israel's neighbors are trying to accomplish, there is no way you can understand the Middle East peace process.

---

[165] http://www.youtube.com/watch?v=XGYxLWUKwWo

[166] http://www.youtube.com/watch?v=QAuBc_cbXo0

[167] http://www.snydertalk.com/?page_id=2760

Yasser Arafat, founder of the Palestine Liberation Organization (PLO), stated the Palestinian position on Israel clearly and concisely:

"Since we cannot defeat Israel in war we do this in stages. We take any and every territory that we can of Palestine, and establish sovereignty there, and we use it as a springboard to take more. When the time comes, we can get the Arab nations to join us for the final blow against Israel." (Yasser Arafat speaking on Jordanian television, September 13, 1993—the same day the Oslo Peace Accord ceremony was held in Washington, D.C.)

Arafat also said,

"Peace for us means the destruction of Israel. We are preparing for an all-out war, a war which will last for generations. Since January 1965, when Fatah was born, we have become the most dangerous enemy that Israel has....We shall not rest until the day when we return to our home, and until we destroy Israel." (El Mundo, Caracas, Venezuela, February 11, 1980)

It doesn't get any clearer than that, and Arafat meant what he said. Nothing that has happened in the Middle East since the PLO was founded or since the Oslo Peace Accord was signed contradicts those statements.

Even though Arafat died in 2004, his philosophies are alive and well. Leaders at all levels in both Hamas and Fatah—the political party that is the major force behind the PLO—continue to push ahead with their plans that they hope and believe will lead to Israel's eventual annihilation. Hamas rules the Gaza Strip and Fatah rules the West Bank. Saying that they don't get along is an understatement. Clandestine operations,

121

murder, and intrigue[168] mark their relationship, but as I said, they agree[169] on one thing. They both hate Israel.

The Palestinian and Hamas Charters paint a portrait of a people wholly committed to one thing—Israel's total destruction. They have a rabid fetish for Israeli blood—particularly the blood of innocent Israeli civilians, and they will be satisfied with nothing less than the elimination of the tiny Jewish homeland in their midst. President Obama, the European Union, and the Quartet can't change that reality, and ignoring it will be the costliest mistake they will ever make.

Israel's Problem is Bigger than Hamas and Fatah

Israel's problem is bigger than Hamas and Fatah. The entire Arab world refuses to recognize Israel's existence. It's true that Israel signed peace treaties with Egypt and Jordan, but the "Arab Spring" proved that those pieces of paper aren't worth very much.

Arabs see Israel as the enemy, and the Arab street is committed to Israel's destruction. Hezbollah, Hamas, Islamic Jihad, the Al Aqsa Martyrs Brigade, and a host of other Islamist groups with menacing names take full advantage of Arab animosity toward Israel, and they use all the resources at their disposal to incite violence against Israel. If you read SnyderTalk (www.snydertalk.com), you know that. What is President Obama's problem? Is he unable to understand what is taking place right in front of his eyes?

---

[168] http://www.youtube.com/watch?v=i9Hga22IWrl

[169] http://www.weeklystandard.com/blogs/damaging-deal-between-hamas-and-fatah_558460.html

Facts about Palestine and "Palestinians"

The Pages in the column on the right of each SnyderTalk post contain a wealth of information with which you should be familiar. One of those pages is titled Facts About Palestine and "Palestinians".[170] Below is some content from that page:

- People we call "Palestinians" today are in large measure descendants of a hodgepodge of unruly Arabs that none of the Arab nations wanted to absorb following Israel's War of Independence in 1948, and for good reason. For instance, Palestinians who migrated to Jordan following Israel's War of Independence created havoc for King Hussein, so he booted them out killing thousands of them in the process during Black September.[171] "Palestinians" then fled to Lebanon and helped to foment the Lebanese Civil War[172] which lasted for more than 15 years and cost untold more lives.

- The Romans changed the name of Israel to Palestine following the Bar Kochba rebellion in 135 B.C.[173] They chose that name to insult Jewish people because the Philistines were Israel's mortal enemies.

- Until 1948, anyone who lived in the country we call Israel today was regarded as a "Palestinian," including Jewish people.[174]

---

[170] http://www.snydertalk.com/?page_id=4062

[171] http://en.wikipedia.org/wiki/Black_September_in_Jordan and http://www.eretzyisroel.org/~samuel/september.html

[172] http://en.wikipedia.org/wiki/Lebanese_Civil_War

[173] http://en.wikipedia.org/wiki/Definitions_of_Palestine_and_Palestinian

[174] http://www.peacefaq.com/palestinians.html

- The number of Jews forced out of Arab countries in 1948 was greater than the number of Arabs who chose to leave "Palestine" for what they thought would be a short time while the Arab nations "drove the Jews into the sea." Since tiny Israel defeated the combined Arab armies, they found themselves homeless.

- Rather than absorb the "Palestinians" who were displaced by the War of Independence, the Arab nations opted instead to set up refugee camps for them. They did this to create squalid living conditions for "Palestinians" in hopes of winning global support for an anti-Israel public relations campaign.[175] It's worth noting that Israel absorbed more than 850,000 Jewish refugees from Arab countries following the War of Independence.[176]

- Yasser Arafat (an Egyptian[177]) commandeered the name "Palestinian" in 1964 when he created the Palestine Liberation Organization (PLO).[178] The primary purpose of the PLO was and is to destroy Israel.[179]

The mainstream media spreads lies about Israel with reckless abandon, and masses of people buy what they are being told. Believers need to prepare for the inevitable confrontations that will result when those lies are exposed. I said "inevitable confrontations" because saving face is of paramount importance to Arabs, and in their world, launching unprovoked attacks against Israel is an acceptable way to save face. It's as though they say, "We don't have anything better to do, so why don't we attack Israel?" That may sound silly, but I think it is very close to the truth—if not the truth.

---

[175] http://www.jewishvirtuallibrary.org/jsource/History/refugees.html

[176] http://www.hsje.org/forcedmigration.htm

[177] http://en.wikipedia.org/wiki/Yasser_Arafat

[178] http://en.wikipedia.org/wiki/Palestine_Liberation_Organization

[179] http://www.snydertalk.com/?page_id=2760

President Obama's Foreign Policy Ineptitude is Evident in the Middle East

Only one thing about President Obama's foreign policy makes any sense. It makes no sense. He's committed to building his own image, and his friends in the media are helping him shape the image that he wants the world to see.

Reality doesn't mesh with the image of our president that they want to project. In the topsy-turvy world of the mainstream media where Obama is concerned, image is substance and indecisiveness is resolve. Today's Western media elites would make George Orwell and Lewis Carroll proud, but the fact still remains that when it comes to foreign policy our president is a klutz.

As I said before, one of President Obama's blunders was a declaration that Israel's 1967 border should be her permanent border. After a loud outcry from Israel and her friends in the US, Obama backpedaled as best he could, but it was no use. The facts contradict his inept explanation that the 1967 border has always been the starting point for negotiations. UN Security Council Resolution 242 says that Israel has a right to defensible borders. It was passed following the Six Day War in 1967, and lots of water has gone under the bridge since then. The articles below provide details about the Israeli border question that any serious person should know:

- Obama's Revisionist History[180]

- What Obama did to Israel[181]

---

[180] http://www.americanthinker.com/2011/05/obamas_revisionist_history.html

[181] http://jewishworldreview.com/cols/krauthammer052711.php3

Unfortunately for Israel, President Obama's blunders have serious real world consequences, and his face-saving maneuvers only make matters worse. We need a president who knows the facts, speaks the truth, and stands by our commitments. Barack Obama is not that person.

According to a Palestinian Authority official,[182] President Obama's Mideast peace offer convinced Palestinians to seek statehood at the UN in September 2011. Jonathan Tobin, executive editor at *Commentary* magazine, agrees. He said[183] that the UN disaster is Obama's fault. There is lots of evidence to support those claims. The Palestinians did an end-run around the agreed upon negotiations with Israel and moved to seek recognition from the UN as an independent state because of President Obama's bumbling approach to US foreign policy. The consequences, although maybe unintentional, will be troublesome for Israel, the US, and the world. Unintended or not, the result is the same. Ineptitude has a price.

Rabbi Chaim Richman understands what's happening in Israel today. In the YouTube video below, he presents a real world perspective that you don't get from the Western media. I hope you take a few minutes to watch it because Rabbi Richman is absolutely correct.

- Rabbi Chaim Richman Answers Obama's Speech in Cairo in 2009[184]

President Obama claims to be a Christian, but everything he has done pertaining to Israel suggests just the opposite. Be that as it may, this much is certain. You can't be pro-Obama and pro-Israel.

---

[182] http://www.haaretz.com/news/diplomacy-defense/pa-official-u-s-mideast-peace-offer-convinced-palestinians-to-seek-statehood-at-un-1.385011

[183] http://www.jewishworldreview.com/0911/tobin.php3

[184] http://www.youtube.com/watch?v=kABvNTatbTU&NR=1

A Palestinian State Won't Work

There are many reasons why a Palestinian state of any sort cannot work, chief among them being that Palestinians lack the prerequisites for a nation: common purpose, the desire to live in peace so its citizens can carry on normal lives and build for a better future, concern about the well-being of their children and posterity, a commitment to law and order, and building an economic infrastructure capable of supporting a thriving economy. These are the basics that any nation must have, and all of them are missing.

- **Common Purpose:** Only one thing unites the people we call "Palestinians" today—the desire to annihilate Israel. If you read the Palestinian and Hamas charters,[185] you can't help but notice that the central tenet in both of them is the animus the Palestinian people have for Israel. The elimination of Israel is the overarching theme in both charters, and the creation of a Pan-Arab[186] nation comes in second. Neither of these guiding principles bodes well for peace with Israel or for building a prosperous Palestinian state.

- **The desire to live in peace so its citizens can carry on normal lives and build for a better future:** Judging by what the Palestinians say they want to achieve, peace with Israel is totally out of the question. In fact, based on what they say, war is inevitable. Both charters call upon Palestinians to dedicate their lives and their wealth to destroying Israel. The Western concept of a "normal life" isn't even hinted at, and a better future by their definition is nothing more than a Middle East with no Israel. If you take them at their word, and there is no reason not to, they have no other vision for a brighter future.

---

[185] http://www.snydertalk.com/?page_id=2760

[186] http://www.britannica.com/EBchecked/topic/878838/Pan-Arabism

- **Concern about the well-being of their children and posterity:** Palestinians raise their children to become martyrs—walking bombs that they can explode among crowds of innocent Israelis. That's not what I say. It's what they say, and it's spelled out clearly in their charters as though it's the only reason Palestinians have children. That's a version of love for children and posterity that Western minds can't fathom, and it's certainly not conducive to building a prosperous and peaceful nation.

- **A commitment to law and order:** The Palestinian government, be it Hamas[187] or Fatah,[188] is notorious for corruption and the whims of despotic rulers. The rule of law isn't even part of their vocabulary. Peaceful and prosperous nations that survive over the long-term must have law and order, and there is no evidence that Palestinians want either.

- **Building an economic infrastructure capable of supporting a thriving economy:** The economic model in place today in the Palestinian community is one of providing labor for a bustling Israeli economy and seeking donations from useful idiots around the world who support their cause, which is to destroy Israel. These two economic characteristics are antithetical to building a flourishing national economy. By definition, Palestinians can't seek to eliminate Israel and at the same time expect to thrive as Israel grows and prospers. Similarly, Palestinians can't hope to achieve economic independence if they position themselves as global beggars. Delusory thinking and hatred are not substitutes for sound economic principles, and they don't lead toward prosperity or peace.

---

[187] http://www.youtube.com/watch?v=nOXbrq8Tbb0

[188] http://www.israelnationalnews.com/News/News.aspx/125722#.Tr2k6UMUq7s

Absent sweeping changes in their thinking, there is no way a Palestinian state will work, and no amount of wishing and hoping for peace and prosperity will compensate for the abiding hatred the Palestinian people have for Israel.

Jewish Support for Obama

A recent Gallup poll[189] showed that Jewish support for President Obama is down to 60%. Obama's support was weakest among Jews who attend synagogue regularly. What do those tidbits of information tell us?

1. They tell us that Jewish people in America still support President Obama by a very wide margin even though he has done more harm to Israel than I would have thought possible.

2. They tell us that Jewish people are uninformed about what's taking place in Israel, an unlikely possibility, or they tell us that they are well-informed and prefer the Obama solution which is to throw Israel under the bus.

3. They tell us that Jewish people who take the Bible seriously have a different opinion about goings-on in Israel than those who don't take the Bible seriously.

The same is true for Christians. People who claim to be Christians but reject everything in the Bible that doesn't square with their opinions are among the first in line to support the Palestinian "cause" which is to destroy Israel completely. I'll be blunt. You are not a Christian if you reject Yahweh's word. The Bible is not a smorgasbord, and Yahweh didn't lay it out like a buffet line and tell us to pick and choose the parts we like and ignore the rest.

---

[189] http://www.jpost.com/JewishWorld/JewishNews/Article.aspx?id=228036

The "Right of Return" is a Deal Stopper

Most people don't have a clue what the "right of return" means. In a nutshell, it means that descendants of so-called "Palestinians" who left their homes when Israel's War of Independence in 1948 began have the right to return to their homes, but this issue is murkier than you can imagine. For instance, consider these facts:

- In 1948 when Israel's War of Independence began, everyone living in the land we call Israel today was referred to as a Palestinian—Jews and Arabs alike.

- Yasser Arafat commandeered the name "Palestinian" for Arabs in 1964 when he founded the PLO as the "sole legitimate representative of the Palestinian people."

- When the British Mandate ended, the land was divided into 2 parts: Israel and Transjordan. Transjordan was supposed to be the Arab state, and Israel was supposed to be the Jewish state. Later, the name "Transjordan" was changed to Jordan. For a more complete explanation, see "A Brief History of Israel and Palestine."[190]

- Jews in Palestine at the time of the War of Independence invited their Arab neighbors to stay and help them build a country. Arab leaders told them to flee immediately because they intended to crush the fledgling Jewish state and, as they put it, "to drive the Jews into the sea." Most of the Arabs departed thinking that they would return in a few days at most and reclaim their homes along with spoils left behind by the defeated Jews. As Yahweh

---

[190] http://www.contenderministries.org/articles/israelhistory.php

would have it, tiny Israel defeated the combined Arab armies, and Arabs who left their homes became refugees.

- Most Arab political leaders decided not to offer citizenship to Arabs who fled Israel. Instead, they built refugee camps for them in hopes of winning global sympathy for their plight. King Hussein of Jordan, King Abdullah's father, made it clear that Arab leaders alone were responsible for the plight of the refugees, but his was a voice in the wilderness. Israel gladly accepted Jewish refugees from Arab countries.

- There were more Jewish refugees from Arab countries during Israel's War of Independence than there were Arab refugees from Israel.

- The value of assets left behind by Jewish refugees from Arab countries far exceeds the value of assets left behind by Arabs who fled Israel.

- Many, if not most, of the so-called "Palestinian refugees" today have no connection whatsoever to people who fled Israel at the time of the War of Independence. For decades, Arab leaders have routinely ousted rabble-rousers from their countries and forced them to join their Arab brothers in "Palestinian" refugee camps. It was a form of exile—like being sent to Siberia in Stalin's Soviet Union.

Every year, Arabs remember Nakba Day. In English it means "the Day of Catastrophe." It refers to Israel's defeat of the combined Arab armies during the War of Independence. In a literal sense, they aren't just remembering the "catastrophe," as they put it. They are hoping and waiting for the day when they can reverse their fortunes and return to the land of Israel, or Eretz Yisrael.

On Nakba Day 2011, Palestinian President Mahmoud Abbas issued a statement saying, "The right of return will remain sacred for every Palestinian who was forced by the Zionist war machine to leave his or her home and land in Palestine. The Palestinians won't succumb to extortion; either we get the home and land peacefully, or we will make sacrifices until we return." As the facts above indicate, that statement is a bald-faced lie, but it sells well in the Arab world and among the liberal, leftwing Western intelligentsia who have bought into the Palestinian cause hook, line, and sinker.

In practical terms, Abbas was saying that the "right of return" is nonnegotiable. Even more, he was saying that Arabs will fight until the bitter end for the "right of return." In absolute terms, the "right of return" is the ultimate deal stopper, because Israel will never accept it and for good reasons. In other words, for Palestinian leaders the "right of return" is a convenient way out of any compromise that may lead to peace with Israel.

Supporting the Creation of a Palestinian State is the same as Funding and Equipping Israel's Avowed Enemies

Mahmoud Zahar, a militant Hamas leader, speaking to the Palestinian news agency Ma'an said[191] that recognizing Israel would "preclude the right of the next generations to liberate the lands (i.e., the land of Israel)," and he wondered aloud, "What will be the fate of the five million Palestinians in the diaspora?" His statements were surprisingly straightforward and revealing.

Hamas and Fatah are two warring Palestinian political factions posing as political parties. They are at odds with each other and with everyone else. The

---

[191] http://www.haaretz.com/news/diplomacy-defense/hamas-accepts-1967-borders-but-will-never-recognize-israel-top-official-says-1.361072

Palestinian Authority is a so-called "moderate" Fatah front group masquerading as the Palestinian government in the West Bank. Hamas, a band of blatantly militant Islamist thugs who terrorize Palestinians in Gaza when they aren't firing rockets and mortars into Israel, holds sway in the Gaza Strip. Their recent reconciliation agreement[192] is nothing but a ploy that's designed to attract global media sympathy and support as they attempt to convince a notoriously ill-informed world that Palestinians are finally ready to govern themselves and to peacefully coexist alongside Israel.

Hamas and the PA want two things:

1. recognition of a Palestinian state from which they can attack Israel with impunity and

2. money and weapons from global benefactors so they can conduct military operations.

Make no mistake. The reconciliation between Hamas and Fatah is a charade, and creating a Palestinian state won't solve any problems. It will only make them worse since both groups have vowed to destroy Israel. Their charters make their objectives clear, and neither group has taken steps to change direction. The only thing that ever changes is the story they peddle to a gullible world.

Will the nations of the world buy the Palestinian lie? Unfortunately, the answer is probably "yes," but rest assured that supporting the creation of a Palestinian state is tantamount to funding and equipping Israel's avowed enemies. The United States should play no part in helping to bring about a Palestinian state on land that Yahweh promised to Israel. He will hold nations accountable for their efforts to interfere with His plan.

---

[192] http://globalpublicsquare.blogs.cnn.com/2011/05/04/does-hamas-fatah-reconciliation-make-peace-more-or-less-likely/

Iran is Instigating Trouble throughout the Middle East

A recent article in the *Tehran Times* titled "US kept bin Laden for long time before killing him: Ahmadinejad"[193] presented Iranian President Mahmoud Ahmadinejad's theory that Osama bin Laden was captured long ago by US forces and held in Pakistan as a prisoner until his death/execution could be used to secure votes for Barack Obama in the upcoming US presidential election. Another article in *The Telegraph* titled "Mahmoud Ahmadinejad 'under a spell', Ayatollah Ali Khamenei says"[194] talks about a constitutional crisis that's developing in Iran following Ahmadinejad's refusal to obey orders from Iran's supreme leader, Ayatollah Khamenei.

Ahmadinejad's precarious situation is exemplified by the fact that Ayatollah Mohammad-Taqi Mesbah-Yazdi, a compadre of the Iranian president who believes in the apocalyptic vision of Shia Islam espoused by Ahmadinejad, is quoted as saying publically, "I've told some of my close friends that I am more than 90 per cent certain that he (Ahmadinejad) has been put under a spell. This is not natural at all. No sane person does such things unless his free will has been taken away .... I do not know if it is hypnotism, a spell or relations with yogis. But there is something wrong."

Iran's political leaders are at an impasse, and President Ahmadinejad is being isolated by the religious men in Iran's political order who hold ultimate sway. The final outcome of the conflict is all but certain. President Ahmadinejad's days are numbered, but in the meantime, Iran's religious elite have finally admitted something that thinking people around the world have known for quite some time. Mahmoud Ahmadinejad is crazy. The religious leaders in Iran suffer from grand delusions as well.

---

[193] http://old.tehrantimes.com/Index_view.asp?code=240771

[194] http://www.telegraph.co.uk/news/worldnews/middleeast/iran/8514929/Mahmoud-Ahmadinejad-under-a-spell-Ayatollah-Misbah-Yazdi-says.html

Regardless of their political differences, Ahmadinejad and his religious bosses agree on one thing. They think Israel has to be "wiped off the map," and they have been working hard to accomplish just that. Their fingerprints are all over the revolutionary upheaval in the Middle East that has been called the "Arab Spring." It's actually a "Persian Spring," but that nuance has escaped the notice of the Western intelligentsia. Iran's goal is to replace secular Muslim leaders in the Middle East with Islamist firebrands who share their conviction that Israel should not exist, and they are succeeding.

The Jewish People are Special to Yahweh

Jeremiah 13: 11 says, "I made the whole household of Israel and the whole household of Judah cling to Me,' declares Yahweh, 'that they might be for Me a people, for renown, for praise and for glory; but they did not listen." There is no getting around the fact that Yahweh created the descendants of Abraham through Isaac and Jacob as a special people.

Through that line came the Messiah who is the personification and the manifestation of Yahweh. He is our Redeemer and our Savior, and He came to do the job that only He could do. He is the greatest blessing the world has ever known, and the Jewish people are a special blessing to the entire world as well. In science, literature, the arts, and in every other field of endeavor, they have made monumental contributions. The magnitude of their contributions dwarfs their size as a group. For instance, between 1901 and 2010, Jewish people or people who are predominantly Jewish accounted for 22% of the Nobel Prizes[195] awarded, but they make up less than 0.2% of the world's population.

---

[195] http://www.jinfo.org/Nobel_Prizes.html

Jewish people are indeed a people of renown, and they were created to bring praise and glory to Yahweh. They haven't always done that, but Yahweh's promises to and about the Jewish people are not dependent on their behavior. Yahweh fulfills His promises despite their shortcomings. They will forevermore cling to Yahweh just as He said. There is no way to prevent it from happening.

Yahweh's promises concerning the Promised Land[196] are just as certain as His promises about the Jewish people. No one will ever be able to change them. Trying to alter those promises in any way or standing in the way of their fulfillment makes no sense because nothing will prevent Yahweh from doing exactly what He said He will do. If the United States or any other nation becomes an obstacle in the path to their fulfillment, they will pay a heavy price.

While it may be politically correct at the present time to talk about the two-state solution as the only path that leads toward peace in the Middle East, just the opposite will happen. It is a path that leads to war and to direct confrontation with Yahweh. It's time to take Yahweh seriously and reject any attempt to divide the Land of Israel.

Jewish People Living in the United States are a Help and a Hindrance to Israel

A very good article by James Lewis appeared in *American Thinker*. It's titled "America's Floating Jews."[197] Lewis tries to explain why President Obama won the election in 2008 and why he continues to get overwhelming support from the US Jewish community despite all the damage he has done to and around Israel. He introduces a concept of Eastern European origin that Jewish people used back in the old country—Luftmensch.[198] According to Lewis, it means "something like 'space cadet.'"

---

[196] http://www.snydertalk.com/?page_id=2490

[197] http://www.americanthinker.com/2011/07/american_jews_are_floating_in_mid-air.html

[198] http://www.merriam-webster.com/dictionary/luftmensch

Polling data indicates that Jewish support for Obama is down from almost 80% to just 70% or 60% depending on the poll you read. What do those statistics tell us?

In a presidential election, a winner who gets 55% of the vote is considered to have won by a "landslide." For instance, Ronald Reagan had a "landslide" victory over Jimmy Carter, but there is no common word that I'm aware of to describe a 70% winner or even a 60% winner. It's almost unheard of at the presidential level. For example, Richard Nixon won in 1972 over George McGovern with 60.7%[199] of the vote, but presidential elections tend to be very close. That's why the overwhelming Jewish support for President Obama is so striking. It suggests that as a group they are not thinking for themselves. They are voting as a block without regard for the facts.

That brings me back to the Luftmensches. Call them space cadets or airheads or dimwits or whatever, they certainly are not enlightened. I call them useful idiots because they are putty in the hands of people like President Obama. They march in lockstep to his drumbeat despite overwhelming evidence that his policies are taking this nation to the edge of a cliff.

Jewish people should know that. They're smart, but they can't seem to break away from their liberal bents even though mountains of evidence tell them that they should. If they ran their businesses the way Obama runs our government, their businesses would fail, and I'm not guessing. That's a fact.

Be that as it may, when any segment of the population supports any candidate at the 70% level or the 60% level, it shows that they are guided by dogma or tradition or something, but not by their brains. Thinking people can see pros and cons on both

---

[199] http://en.wikipedia.org/wiki/United_States_presidential_election,_1972

sides of an issue, but mind-numb robots can't. All they can see are their prejudices, and they vote accordingly.

Will Jewish People Continue to Support Barack Obama in 2012

Trying to lure[200] Jewish voters back into the Democratic fold, President Obama went so far as to offer them private access to him. I guess he wants them to think that they are on the same level as executives in companies like Solyndra, for example, but that's just speculation.

An interesting article in *Haaretz* titled "Obama tells Jewish donors that U.S.-Israel disagreements are only 'tactical'"[201] was revealing. It was about a speech that President Obama gave to an audience of potential Jewish donors to his 2012 presidential campaign. As the title indicates, the president told the assembled Jews that any policy differences between the US and Israel are only "tactical." He went on to say that the U.S. and Israel "will always be stalwart allies and friends." As you would expect, since the president was there to pick their pockets, he explained how important the Jewish donors in the room are to him and his administration:

> "But it's going to require some hard work, and it's going to require that not only this administration employs all of its creative powers to try to bring about peace in the region, but it's also going to require all of you as engaged citizens of the United States who are friends of Israel making sure that you are giving us suggestions, you are in an honest dialogue with us, that you're helping to shape how both Americans and Israelis think about the opportunities and challenges."

---

[200] http://www.worldjewishdaily.com/obama-jews.php

[201] http://www.haaretz.com/news/diplomacy-defense/obama-tells-jewish-donors-that-u-s-israel-disagreements-are-only-tactical-1.368864

The gist of the article points to the fact that Jewish donors are not getting "cold feet" when it comes to supporting President Obama in 2012 and suggests that things are just hunky-dory between the Obama administration and the American Jewish community. Is that conclusion accurate? Only time will tell.

This much I do know. Jewish people in the US made a terrible mistake when they supported candidate Obama in 2008. As president, Barack Obama has done more damage to Israel than anyone could have imagined while he was running for office. His snubs of Prime Minister Netanyahu reveal his deep-seated animosity for Israel's elected leader and for the Israeli people who elected him. But Obama's hostility toward Israel runs deeper than that. His view of the Middle East is relentlessly slanted toward Arab Muslims. His Cairo speech[202] in 2009 shows the lengths to which he will go to win their homage and tossing Israel under the bus is not too high a price for him to pay.

Having completed almost three years of his 4-year term, this much is clear. President Obama has turned his back on Israel and cost the Israeli people dearly, but despite the preferential treatment he has given Arab Muslims, he is vilified in their world. He can't win for losing.

Watching our president attempting to position himself to take some credit for the "Arab Spring" would have been comical if it weren't so pathetic, and the foolishness isn't over yet. It's difficult to understand what potential Jewish donors might detect in President Obama's record that would lead them to believe he is Israel's friend. Let's hope and pray that Jewish people in the United States and the rest of the world can see clearly through the haze in 2012.

---

[202] http://www.huffingtonpost.com/2009/06/04/obama-speech-in-cairo-vid_n_211215.html

President Obama is not Israel's friend no matter what he says. His actions give him away. The most effective things Jewish people can do to send President Obama a message are to withhold their financial support and to vote for his opponent.

It's Delusional to believe that Israel is the Problem in the Middle East

I've been a strong supporter of Israel for as long as I can remember, but my attitude toward Israel changed dramatically when I started taking the Bible seriously. That was about 40 years ago. Based on what the Bible says, it's patently absurd to say that you are for Yahweh and against Israel, and as I've said before, you can't be pro-Obama and pro-Israel. If you read the Bible and pay attention to Yahweh's promises about the Promised Land,[203] you can't deny that the Scriptures make it clear that the Promised Land belongs to Abraham's descendants through Isaac and Jacob.

It's delusional to believe that Israel is an obstacle to peace in the Middle East. Both the Palestinian and Hamas charters call for Israel's annihilation, and Palestinian leaders, be they Hamas or Fatah, still preach Israel's destruction to their children. "Palestinians" as a people are wholly committed to the eradication of the State of Israel, and it's delusional to believe otherwise.

That brings me to Dennis Ross, President Obama's chief Middle East advisor. Speaking in Jerusalem during the "Arab Spring," he told a group of prominent Israelis that "doing nothing" at a time of "sweeping change" in the Middle East is the wrong policy for Israel to adopt.

Doing nothing? What was Ross talking about?

---

[203] http://www.snydertalk.com/?page_id=2490

Israel turned over Gaza to the Palestinians in 2005, and Gazans gave the reins of power to Hamas in 2006. Since that fateful day, Israel has endured an unrelenting barrage of terrorist attacks emanating from Gaza. In the mid-1990s, Israel started turning over towns in the West Bank to the Palestinians including Hebron, Shechem, and Jenin, and they quickly became breeding grounds for radical Islamist malcontents who have committed their lives to killing Jews. Israel provided weapons to Palestinian security forces, and they found their way into the hands of terrorists who used them to attack innocent Israeli men, women, and children. To this day, Israel funnels tax revenue to the Palestinians which they use to fund terrorist attacks on Israel. That's not "nothing." It's foolish and shortsighted, but it isn't "nothing."

Following the Wye River Summit in October 1998, Ross (who worked for President Bill Clinton at the time) insisted that the Palestinians remove the articles in their charter calling for Israel's destruction. Yasser Arafat, who was Palestinian president at the time, dutifully assembled a group of people who posed for the cameras and voted to abolish the articles in question. Problem is they were not members of the Palestinian National Council—the only group authorized to change the Palestinian Charter. It was a charade, but Ross was thrilled with the outcome. He wrote about it nostalgically in his 2005 book *The Missing Peace: The Inside Story of the Fight for Middle East Peace.*

After that heralded vote, Muammar Kaddafi summoned Arafat to Libya to explain what happened. Arafat assured Kaddafi that nothing had changed, that the vote was merely an attempt to placate Bill Clinton. Even so, 7 years after the vote and after serious policy experts pointed out the deception, Ross wrote about it in his book as though it was a significant achievement. That's a perfect example of delusion. Psychiatrists refer to it as delusional disorder: "false beliefs based on incorrect inference about external reality that persist despite the evidence to the contrary."[204]

---

[204] http://emedicine.medscape.com/article/292991-overview

The delusion about peace in the Middle East is that Israel is the problem. Nothing could be further from the truth. Barack Obama, Hillary Clinton, Dennis Ross, and the entire Obama team are deluded beyond belief. Their misguided policies have done untold damage to our only real ally in the Middle East and maybe the world. Still, Obama and his sycophants continue to reject the facts while they push an agenda that is dangerous to both the US and Israel.

Yahweh's promises and commitments haven't changed one iota, and they never will. In the end, He will win. I'm on Yahweh's side. Which side are you on? Only a fool bets against a sure winner.

Below is a very short list of recent news headlines dealing with the Middle East. Simply scanning the headlines and googling a few of the articles will give you some idea what Israel is up against:

- Syria warns against UN censure

- 48 reported killed as Syria forces continue attacks on protesters

- White House calls for 'immediate end' to Syria violence

- Could Assad vent his wrath on Israel?

- Egypt must resist relapse to despotism

- As Islamists Flex Muscle, Egypt's Christians Despair

- Gaddafi forces kill 22 rebels in Misrata shelling

- Libyan rebels repel fierce attack by government forces on Misrata

- Haniyeh: No differences among Hamas leaders

- 'Iran caught 10 times trying to send arms to terrorists'

- 'PA bans journalists from reporting human rights abuses'

- Lebanese Hezbollah Fighters Being Used By Syrian Regime To Put Down Rebellion

- Hezbollah chief: Naksa Day protesters sent clear message to Israel

- Palestine – An Arab West Bank Is A Lost Cause

- Thousands in Yemen's capital push for ouster of president

- Yemeni Warplanes Strike Militants in Seized Town

- FBI Director: Al Qaeda Remains Committed to Attacking U.S.

- Saudi attacks linked to al-Qaeda team

- Who Is the Middle East's Biggest Loser from the Arab Revolutions?

Chapter 8

President Obama Thinks and Acts like a Child

Childish behavior is something we don't want or need in our president, and Barack Obama has behaved childishly since the day he took office. At home and abroad, he has disgraced himself and our country with his juvenile antics. Unfortunately, he seems to be unaware of his problem, but leaders around the world are. So are people in this country—everyone who isn't an Obamanista, that is.

I'm not a psychiatrist or a psychologist, so I won't make any attempt to psychoanalyze the president. I'll leave it to professionals to try and figure out the root cause of Obama's problem, but as a citizen of the United States, a taxpayer, and a person who cares deeply about the effects of our nation's policies on people in other countries, I think I have a duty and a responsibility to address the problems I see— problems that are readily apparent. The issues we face as a nation and as a world are too important and the risks are too great to place them in the hands of a juvenile or a person who thinks and acts like one.

What Should We Look for in a President?

Some will argue, correctly I might add, that everyone behaves childishly on occasion. I've done it myself and so have you, but childishness is not the norm for adults or for people who think like adults. It's certainly not the norm for presidents, or it shouldn't be. Adolescent behavior is an everyday occurrence for President Obama, even in his dealings with leaders of other nations.

It's also true that politicians at every level of government behave childishly all the time. If you read newspapers or watch the news on television, you know that. Some will argue that it's not fair to single out President Obama for criticism for doing what most politicians do, but that argument falls flat because the presidency is not just another political office. It's the highest office in the land—a land that is the world's lone superpower. The fact that many if not most politicians behave childishly is not a good argument for electing as president a man who routinely thinks and acts like a child.

Our goal should be to weed out the adolescents and to select the most intelligent, the most mature, the most experienced, the most honest, and the wisest people we can find to lead this nation. Based on those criteria, Barack Obama is not qualified to be president. Nothing that President Obama has done during his first 3 years in office suggests that he is even near the top of the list in any of those areas. In fact, his actions as president indicate that he may be near the bottom of the list. Some in the Obamanista camp are even beginning to wonder publicly if they would have been better off with Hillary Clinton as president. That should tell you something.

Inexperience is not a Qualification for the Presidency

For good reasons, to become eligible for the job of president, being elected to high political office previously is a near must. Rarely is a person elected president who hasn't served in public office before. When it happens, it's because he did something extraordinarily well—people like Dwight Eisenhower for example. He was the Supreme Commander of Allied Forces in Europe during World War II. His achievements speak for themselves, but Barack Obama's record isn't exemplary in any area, and it never has been. In fact, you can even say that prior to being elected president Obama's only significant political accomplishment was getting elected to the United States Senate, and he certainly didn't make a mark there.

Obama spent his entire 4 years in the Senate running for president. He didn't have time as a senator to do anything noteworthy, and he didn't even try because it would have interfered with his primary pursuit—getting elected president. There is a huge difference between holding political office and having political experience, and President Obama's lack of political experience has been a major problem for the United States since he took office. But his childishness has been an even bigger problem.

As the title of this book suggests, I believe President Obama was elected president for just one reason. He is a black man, or more precisely he's a half black man, who managed to become a United States senator, and he has a folksy style that makes him an attractive stump speaker. Those were and still are his major "qualifications" for office, but they are not sufficient to qualify him for the highest office in the land. After 3 years in office, I think it's fair to say that President Obama hasn't learned very much, and it's time for us to correct the mistake we made as a nation when we elected him president.

Evidences of President Obama's Juvenile Behavior

I'll focus my attention on the childish behaviors below:

- a tendency to throw tantrums,

- pettiness,

- being overly opinionated,

- a tendency to talk too much,

- arrogance, and

- refusing to accept responsibility.

A Tendency to Throw Tantrums

At the White House in July 2011 during the budget debate, President Obama had a tantrum when Republicans challenged him on specific budget issues. Finally, the president said, "Enough is enough. Don't call my bluff. I'm going to the American people."[205]

There's nothing wrong with the president getting angry and there's nothing wrong with him going to the American people, but there is a problem when he can't even discuss ideas without throwing a fit. Obama's tendency to talk down to members of Congress who disagree with him and his tantrums are getting us nowhere fast.

In August 2011 when Standard & Poor's downgraded US bonds, the president went off the deep end. In a fit of rage, he said in essence that the Standard & Poor's decision "smacked of an institution starting with a conclusion and shaping any arguments to fit it."[206] I addressed the Standard & Poor's downgrade in chapter 2, and the president's assessment is ridiculous. If President Obama had kept his cool and tried to understand what the rating agency was telling him, he would have been more willing to address our deficit and debt problems and there would have been no downgrade. The cost to the United States for our president's childish tantrum is high and rising.

Pettiness

President Obama has bowed and scraped before the Muslim world, and he has humiliated himself on more than one occasion in the process—even though he didn't

---

[205] http://www.washingtontimes.com/news/2011/jul/15/pruden-obamas-tantrum-in-a-high-chair/

[206] http://www.washingtontimes.com/news/2011/aug/8/obamas-tantrum-against-sp/

realize it. At the same time, the president has bent over backwards to humiliate and ridicule two of our staunchest allies: Israel and Great Britain. Why? It's because he's a petty person, and he has some pent-up anger that he can't control.

The list of President Obama's snubs of Great Britain is very long, but the article titles below will make my case. Google them and see what I mean:

- Barack Obama sends bust of Winston Churchill on its way back to Britain

- Barack Obama snubs British scientists by refusing to receive Royal Society medal

- Barack Obama snubs Britain by saying France is his biggest ally

- Barack Obama snubs Gordon Brown over private talks

- Obama snubs Queen Elizabeth

President Obama has also gone out of his way to snub Israel's Prime Minister Benyamin Netanyahu as the article titles below show. You need to google them as well:

- Binyamin Netanyahu humiliated after Barack Obama 'dumped him for dinner'

- Behind the scenes: Obama snubs Netanyahu

Regardless of Obama's personal feelings toward Israel and Great Britain, he is the President of the United States, and he has an obligation to treat our allies with respect. The cost of treating them poorly can be very high. I'm almost embarrassed to have to say that because I believe a person with even marginal intelligence should know it without being told. Enough said. By the same token, it makes no sense to bow and scrape before our enemies and ne'er-do-well friends. That should go without saying too.

Being Overly Opinionated

The fact that President Obama is opinionated is the stuff of legend after only 3 short years in office. The following examples prove my point:

- The Obamacare Disaster[207]
- Another green-energy debacle shows Obama's folly[208]

Healthcare and green energy are two areas where President Obama thinks he has made valuable contributions to our country, but mountains of hard evidence say just the opposite. And why do we have Obamacare and unfocused green energy boondoggles at the expense of coal, oil, and natural gas. There is only one reason. Barack Obama has an opinion and nothing else matters. The cost of an overly opinioned president is very high. Green energy and Obamacare prove that fact.

Talks too much

I believe that anyone who thinks President Obama doesn't talk too much should have his head examined. It's getting to the point where he's the butt of jokes even among Democrats. Problem is when you say too much and you have nothing new to

---

[207] http://spectator.org/archives/2010/08/18/the-obamacare-disaster

[208] http://www.dispatch.com/content/stories/editorials/2011/09/04/another-green-energy-debacle-shows-obamas-folly.html

say, people stop taking you seriously. I reached that point with Obama a long time ago. The examples below suggest that I'm not alone:

- Does Obama talk too much for his own good?[209]

- The President Talks Too Much[210]

- It's all Obama, all the time[211]

Arrogance

As a part of President Obama's bow and scrape pony show, he told the world that the United States has been arrogant. Maybe we have been a little arrogant, but that's not the issue here. The point is that Barack Obama is probably the most arrogant president the United States has ever had. I'll say this much for the president, though. The list of people who think he's arrogant crosses party lines, and it extends to countries around the globe. Google the articles below and see what I mean:

- Musharraf: Obama is arrogant

- Rove Rips 'Arrogant' Obama's Carter Comparison

- Perry calls Obama 'arrogant' on Israel

- Barack Obama's Arrogant Marxist Rhetoric

---

[209] http://www.marketwatch.com/story/does-president-obama-talk-to-us-too-much-2009-07-24

[210] http://www.cato.org/pub_display.php?pub_id=10000

[211] http://www.politico.com/news/stories/0409/21286.html

Refusing to Accept Responsibility

There are so many examples of President Obama refusing to accept responsibility that I hardly know where to begin. Thus, I decided to zero in on just one because it is so telling—the Gunwalker scandal. The article titles below make that clear. They make for some interesting reading:

- Gunwalker: Details of Coverup Revealed

- Gunwalker Explodes into the Heartland

- Gunwalker Explodes: FBI Hid Weapon, Tax Dollars Subsidized Murder

- Gunwalker Scandal Escalates: Grenadewalker?

- Gunwalker's Body Count Grows, Along with the Obama Administration's Cover-Up

Gunwalker, a.k.a. Fast and Furious, is a program set up by the U.S. Bureau of Alcohol, Tobacco, and Firearms (ATF) that encouraged gun shops in the United States to sell thousands of assault rifles and other weapons to Mexican drug cartels—not directly, but through middlemen—so US law enforcement officials could learn about the flow pattern. The program turned out to be a catastrophe, and the number of lives lost in the process is high and rising.

The ATF manager of the program says[212] that he shared information about Gunwalker with the White House, but President Obama denies[213] knowing anything

---

[212] http://www.cbsnews.com/8301-31727_162-20083772-10391695.html

[213] http://www.humanevents.com/article.php?id=45398

about it. Mexican officials are furious[214] about Fast and Furious, and they should be. Representative Darrell Issa (R-California) says that the Obama administration is gaming[215] the system and denying information about Gunwalker to House investigative committees.

No one in government who has even a smidgen of sense believes that President Obama didn't know about the Gunwalker program. I'll go one step further. If everyone in the White House knew about Gunwalker except the president, that's a bigger problem than Obama knowing about it and saying he didn't.

This is the bottom line. The United States faces some of the most daunting challenges we've ever faced as a nation, and a child is leading us. Technically, he's an adult, but he thinks and acts like a small boy. President Obama's tendency to throw tantrums, his pettiness, his dogmatic ways, his tendency to talk too much, his arrogance, and his repeated refusals to accept responsibility for his actions are compelling reasons not to vote for him in 2012.

---

[214] http://www.thenewamerican.com/world-mainmenu-26/north-america-mainmenu-36/9064-mexican-officials-furious-over-atf-gunrunning

[215] http://www.youtube.com/watch?v=3WnXANaE27o&feature=related

Chapter 9

The Conclusion:
It's Time for Change We Can Really Believe In

In September 2011, Dick Morris, a political consultant and an advisor to President Clinton, wrote an interesting op-ed piece titled "Obama might pull out."[216] Below are three quotes from Morris' piece:

- "As bad news piles up for the Democrats, I asked a top Democratic strategist if it were possible that President Obama might 'pull a Lyndon Johnson' and soberly face the cameras, telling America that he has decided that the demands of partisan politics are interfering with his efforts to right our economy and that he has decided to withdraw to devote full time to our recovery. His answer: 'Yes. It's possible. If things continue as they are and have not turned around by January, it is certainly possible.'"

- "Obama's historic race to the top in 2008 was animated by huge margins and turnouts among four key groups: African-Americans, Hispanics, Jews and young voters. New polling data and the results of the Brooklyn-Queens Turner-Weprin elections suggest that his base is decaying, chunk by chunk."

- "Only the African-Americans remain of Obama's 2008 coalition. Surveys show his approval among blacks at higher than 80 percent, indicating no diminution of his enthusiasm there."

---

[216] http://www.jewishworldreview.com/0911/morris092111.php3

It's possible that President Obama might pull out of the 2012 presidential campaign. That would be good for America, but I wouldn't count on it if I were you since he has done nothing in 3 years that's good for America. Assuming that he'll start now makes no sense. Keep in mind that President Obama owns the bully pulpit and he has control of the purse strings until he leaves office. Those are powerful tools that he can use at his discretion. Don't assume that he will just throw in the towel. If we think that he will pull out and then he doesn't, we will lose because we will let our guards down. That would be a terrible mistake.

Obama Doesn't Have a Strategy[217]

One thing stands out in my mind about President Obama's so-called "budget strategy." He doesn't have one. You can see evidence of Mr. Obama's strategic vacuum in everything he does. Take the much ballyhooed budget speech he gave at George Washington University in April 2011, for example. It contradicted the message he delivered as a part of his 10-year budget just a few short weeks earlier. All of the evidence points to the fact that Obama's "budget strategy" was simply a kneejerk reaction to Representative Paul Ryan's (R-Wisconsin) budget proposal which really does reflect strategic thinking. It's been said, and it's true, that talk is cheap. Talk seems to be the only arrow in Mr. Obama's quiver.

The president's speech droned on for about an hour and when it was over, the most memorable thing about it was its lack of specificity. The phrase "my plan," which he used repeatedly is not a substitute for specifics, and the examples he used to support his "plan" were woefully inadequate. Take infrastructure spending, for instance. The president explained that he would spend on infrastructure. Who's against that? No one.

---

[217] http://www.americanthinker.com/2011/04/obamas_strategy_he_doesnt_have.html

Problem is infrastructure spending was supposed to be the primary focus of his stimulus package. At the beginning of his presidency, we were told about the "shovel-ready projects" that would get us out of the Great Recession and fix our crumbling roads and bridges in the process. Three years and hundreds of billions of dollars later, what does the record show? We still have crumbling roads and bridges, precious little construction work, and more deficits and debt than any generation of Americans has ever seen with more to come. That's not strategy. It's business as usual. Paraphrasing Albert Einstein, "The quality of thinking that got us here won't get us out of here."

If the president had a strategy for dealing with our deficit and debt problems, he would have presented it long ago—in detail. He could have used his budget commission's plan to get our fiscal house in order as the launching pad to introduce his strategy, and he would have if he had one. President Obama's silence at that critical moment was deafening, and his April 2011 speech was nothing more than an attempt to avoid the appearance of incompetence—a trick that is becoming increasingly difficult for him to pull off even among his once ardent supporters.

Mr. Obama's strategic void has also been on display in the Middle East since the Arab Spring began in January 2011. For instance, consider Egypt. Obama stood with our long-time ally, Hosni Mubarak, and then he didn't. Then he stood with him again until the political winds shifted, at which point Obama announced that it was time for Mr. Mubarak to go. Our president demonstrated the same lack of strategic resolve on matters related to Syria, Libya, Tunisia, Bahrain, Yemen, Iran, and Saudi Arabia. Our president's inability to grasp strategic concepts is so pervasive that the King of Saudi Arabia said[218] recently that President Obama is a threat to Saudi Arabia's internal security. I think he's a threat to our internal security as well.

---

[218] http://www.washingtonpost.com/opinions/amid-the-arab-spring-obamas-dilemma-over-saudi-arabia/2011/04/07/AFhILDxC_story.html

Mr. Obama did have a strategy for getting elected to the highest office in the land, but it wasn't his. Whose plan it was remains a mystery, as does almost everything else about our president from the hospital where he was born to his SAT and LSAT scores to his academic performance records to his golf handicap. Even so, the facts are beginning to emerge. Take his first autobiography, for example. Jack Cashill's *Deconstructing Obama* suggests strongly that Obama didn't write it and that Bill Ayers probably did.

It's looking a lot like someone or some group carefully orchestrated a comprehensive strategy to take an obscure Illinois lawyer specializing in community organizing from nowhere to the White House. That plan will go down in the annals of history as a strategic masterpiece—a stroke of genius. No one deft enough to devise a scheme for Obama's political ascension could be so strategically clumsy in office. Barack Obama is not a strategist. At best, he's a skillful opportunist.

The "I have a Plan" Mantra is no Substitute for a Plan

When John Kerry ran for president against George Bush in 2008, his "I have a plan" mantra was tiresome to the point of being noxious. According to him, he had a plan for everything. I heard that slogan so often that I started mocking him, something I'm prone to do when dimwit politicians lie through their teeth to voters who should know better.

As irksome as it was for me to hear Kerry say, "I have a plan", it infuriates me even more when a sitting president, Barack Obama, says "I'll have a plan in a few days or weeks." Obama's been President of the United States for almost 3 years. When He took office, our economy was in desperate straits—he says so all the time. He was given carte blanche by Congress to get the economy moving again. He's already spent trillions of our hard-earned dollars supposedly to create jobs and jumpstart the US economic engine. Now with just over a year to go in office, I hope, he keeps laying out "new" plans that aren't new and telling us that he'll come up more plans in the future.

Who's Obama trying to kid? Does he think we're idiots? His own National Commission on Fiscal Responsibility and Reform gave him a plan which he summarily rejected. Representative Paul Ryan presented a plan that he mocked and ridiculed. All the while, our "tireless" president who isn't getting enough sleep, we are told, because he spends so much time and energy trying to figure out how to create jobs, has been a nonentity in the process.

President Obama has done three things for which he will always be remembered:

1. He shoved Obamacare down our throats.

2. He paid off his union supporters from the 2008 election with our tax dollars.

3. He has stifled economic activity in every sector of the economy with regulations that make no sense to anyone who isn't a part of his leftwing cabal. When Congress stood in his way, he just issued another executive order. We call that "ruling by fiat," and it's just one step away from dictatorship.

In President Obama's case, this old cliché is true: the emperor has no clothes. Between now and the 2012 election, the American people will be best served by our president if he will just get out of the way and let the adults get the job done, but that's wishful thinking on my part. It's not going to happen. Until Obama is defeated at the polls, he will remain an obstacle to progress.

At long last, Congress is trying to move in the right direction. If it were not for liberals in the Senate, we would have gotten a debt and deficit deal that would have precluded the US bond downgrade by Standard & Poor's. Which side did President Obama support in that charade? If you think he supported the side of fiscal responsibility and reform, you need to have your head examined.

Our president has no idea what fiscal responsibility and reform mean. He lives in a dream world with sugarplum fairies who grant wishes and no one has to pay for anything—ever. Harry Reid, Nancy Pelosi, and their lackluster lackeys have the same dream, but to the rest of America and the world, it's a nightmare.

It's Time for Hope and Change that We Can Really Believe In

The United States has had enough of President Obama. His policies relating to the economy, the environment, healthcare, justice, and a host of other issues have caused great harm in this country; they are stifling job creation; and they are leading us to a debt and deficit crisis from which recovery will be very difficult.

President Obama's enthusiasm for deficit spending despite our alarming debt problem is mindboggling. His penchant for ruling by decree, although not unprecedented in American history, undermines the very foundations of our democracy. After almost 3 years in office, like an adolescent child Obama continues to blame his predecessor for problems that he was elected to solve, many of which he created.

When President Obama took office, his chief of staff, Rahm Emanuel, said, "Never let a crisis go to waste," and that line became his governing principle. With the complicity of a Democratic House and a Democratic Senate, his first maneuver as president was to remake our healthcare system in the socialist image that he so admires. State after state has attempted to block his plan because they know that the responsibility for paying the bill for his misguided initiative will eventually fall into their laps. Federal courts so far have sided with the states, but the jury is still out on the fate of Obamacare. An election is needed to lay that issue to rest.

At the beginning of his administration, President Obama wasted his time and the time of the US Congress on his massive healthcare overhaul, time that he and they could have and should have used to get our economy moving. More than any other president in modern history, Obama was given carte blanche by his Democratic comrades in the House and Senate to spend trillions of dollars of our money to bring our economy back from the precipice. Instead, he devoted all of his efforts to socializing medicine and propping up unions that have contributed mightily to our debt and deficit problems.

On the global stage, President Obama has been a disaster as well. He has thumbed his nose at our friends and cozied up to our enemies. Israel in particular has been the target of his animosity, and he has showered Israel's enemies with praise and our hard-earned tax dollars.

Even Obama's friends in the Democratic Party have had difficulty explaining his foreign policy initiatives. Trying to cast his ploys in a positive light, they described his bungling moves as "dithering" and "leading from behind." Leading from behind isn't leading at all, and dithering is evidence that President Obama is hopelessly lost in a world that he can't fathom. The American people are beginning to accept the truth, and it's showing up in the polls.

President Obama is a narcissist. When he says, "This is not about me," he really means "this is all about me." Obama's first and some would say his only priority is to look like something he is not—a great president. He's not even a good president. When historians weigh in on the Obama presidency, they will treat him the same way they have treated Jimmy Carter, and for good reasons. Carter is the president most like President Obama.

159

Obama and His Cabal are Destroying Our Nation

In July 2011, former House Speaker Nancy Pelosi was caught on an open microphone saying, "The Republicans are trying to destroy this country as we know it." What is Pelosi for? What things does she think are threatened by the GOP?

- Socialized medicine that we didn't and don't want—a poor substitute for what we had prior to Obamacare and a healthcare system that will sink this nation under a mountain of debt.

- Abortion on demand with no restraints whatsoever.

- Perversity in a myriad of forms.

- Irresponsible spending on everything under the sun with no regard for the consequences.

- Carbon emissions standards that will change this country in ways that most people can't even imagine in order to accomplish absolutely nothing except to make people like Al Gore rich.

I could go on listing items on Pelosi's agenda, but the list above should suffice. She thinks the Republicans are trying to change all of these things. Truth be told, some of them are and some of them are not. Despite the posturing taking place in Washington right now thanks to our deficit, debt, and jobs problems, many Republicans are firmly in Pelosi's camp. I would love to see voters in their districts give them the heave-ho in 2012 along with President Obama. Who knows? Maybe they will.

Then there are Republicans and a few Democrats too who realize that we are on an unsustainable path—a path that leads to destruction. They are opposed to most of the things on Pelosi's and Obama's agenda, and they should be.

Voters will have a chance to make their voices heard again in November 2012. The tide is turning against Pelosi, Obama, and Harry Reid. We may yet have an opportunity to right the ship and build for a more prosperous future, but that is by no means certain. It depends on people like you and me.

We live in perilous times. Have we reached the tipping point, the point of no return? I don't know, but if we haven't, you can see it from here.

Our Deficit and Debt Problems Must be Solved

Our nation's debt and deficit problems weren't solved by raising the debt ceiling, and the 2012 presidential election is the place to fight the real war on deficits and debt. I used the word "war" instead of "battle" or "fight" to describe what comes next because that's where we are politically. Why? It's because our Congress and presidents from both parties have given us an irresponsible government that is willing to spend like there will be no tomorrow, but they are unwilling to pay for what they want to buy.

This is the bottom line. We spend too much money—way too much money, but that's not all. About 50% of our fellow citizens pay no federal income taxes. They are freeloaders who take but don't give. In a representative republic like ours, that's an enormous problem.

This isn't a political statement, although some will argue that it is. The Democratic Party is THE PARTY that the freeloaders among us support by a margin of

161

roughly 99.9% to approximately 0.1%. It's the party that stands for abortion on demand without restraint, perversity of all sorts, paying people to do nothing from generation to generation, and spending without regard for the willingness or the ability to pay. Don't get me wrong. Some Republicans are just as irresponsible as Democrats, but they don't represent an overwhelming majority of the party.

Right now, at this very moment, we have deficit and debt crises, but they're not the real problem. The real problem is the irresponsible people we have elected and continue to elect. That makes us, the electorate, responsible. As I said, almost half of us are freeloading, so we face a problem of gargantuan proportions that will take some time to solve. But solve it we must because if we don't this country won't survive. As I said, the 2012 presidential election is the right place to fight the war on deficits and debt—out in the open for all to see.

It's Time to Get Serious and Solve our Problems

Barack Obama's behavior as president reminds me of an adolescent child. He wants things his way, and he'll pitch a fit if he doesn't get what he wants when he wants.

Take Obamacare, for instance. He wanted to redesign our healthcare system to make it more...something. He didn't care what doctors and other healthcare professionals said. Instead, he relied on people like Barney Frank and Nancy Pelosi to fill in the details and impose the healthcare system they wanted on the rest of us. At the same time, every socialist fringe group in this nation of ours got things they wanted at our expense, and friends of Obama who didn't like the plan have been given waivers. If that's not adolescent behavior, I don't know what is.

162

What about energy? Obama told the editors at the *San Francisco Chronicle* that if he was elected president he would impose high costs on energy producers that didn't go along with his nebulous "green energy agenda" and energy prices would "necessarily skyrocket." That's one promise he has kept. Gas and electricity prices are rapidly rising because Obama's EPA and other government agencies that he controls are imposing restrictive regulations on energy producers by fiat. Never mind that Congress and energy professionals think that Obama's energy initiatives make no sense. He simply ignores them, drafts executive orders, and tells his henchmen in government to move ahead with his plan anyway. What kind of behavior is that?

The auto industry is another example. Obama used the financial crisis gripping the nation when he assumed office to take control of General Motors, pay off the unions that helped him get elected, and install an executive team at GM that marched to the beat of his drum. In turn, they gave the American people the Chevy Volt. It's a very small and very expensive car that average Americans can't afford to buy. That doesn't matter, though, because it's too small for the average American family anyway. The private sector has a nasty habit of trying to figure out what consumers want, need, and are willing to pay for before they go out on a limb by making big investments in new product ideas. Obama skips that step and simply imposes on the market what he wants consumers to have. That said, I'm encouraged by the fact that both of the people who have dug deep into their pockets to buy a Volt say they like it, and both cars have Obama stickers on the rear bumper. I've never seen one on the highway, and I doubt I ever will.

To put a fine point on it, President Obama's approach to the entire US economy is adolescent. He knows what's best for everybody; he'll tell us what we are going to do whether we like it or not; and if you don't like it, tough. "Me, me, me" should have been Obama's campaign slogan in 2008 because that's exactly what he has delivered as president, but does the president actually know what he's doing. Look at the facts. Unemployment is high and rising; job growth in the private sector is anemic and there are no signs of improvement in the immediate future; Standard & Poor's downgraded US bonds; and traditional buyers of US bonds have taken a hike. If you think these are signs that we are on the right economic path, you need to have your head examined. The time for blaming George Bush is over. This is Obama's economy. His fingerprints are all over it. It's time to blame Obama.

Domestic examples of Obama's adolescent behavior are seemingly endless, but I'll stop there and focus on the Middle East. Our president knows exactly what Israel needs to do to achieve peace. All the Israelis have to do is give up more land to their avowed enemies who have dedicated their lives to Israel's annihilation. Obama knows that will solve the problem. In his universe, the Gaza Strip, Shechem, Hebron, and other towns in the West Bank that Israel gave to the Palestinians are perfect examples of the kind of peace that Israel can expect. Regular, indiscriminate rocket and mortar attacks on innocent Israeli civilians and turning Palestinian controlled areas into terrorist training camps are a small price for the people of Israel to pay for the kind of peace the President Obama envisions. I suspect that he would have a different opinion if he had to raise his family in a world like the one he wants to impose on Israel, but that's the way adolescents are.

President Obama's childish behavior hasn't worked to the advantage of Egypt, Bahrain, Yemen, and Saudi Arabia, for example, either, but the Muslim Brotherhood, Syrian President Bashar al-Assad, and other Israel haters have taken full advantage of Obama's ineptness to strengthen their positions. Obama's lackluster performance on the global stage is becoming the stuff of legend. My guess is that our president thinks he'll leave a legacy that he'll be proud of, but facts suggest otherwise. Not to worry, though, because adolescents can't see beyond their immediate concerns. Saying that Obama is narcissistic is an understatement.

The United States is in Serious Trouble on Multiple Fronts

The deficit is spiraling out of control; our debt load is destroying our credit rating; Congress is clueless; we've turned our back on our only ally in the Middle East and maybe our only friend in the world—Israel; we've done everything but kiss the behinds of radical Islamist rouge states and their donor state brethren; and President Obama is asleep at the switch. Oh, I'm sorry, I meant to say that he's leading from behind.

If you can see through the Obama smokescreen, you know that our country is in serious trouble on multiple fronts. People who haven't downed a glass of Kool-Aid yet are tempted to think that the 2012 presidential election will be a cakewalk for whoever Obama's opponent turns out to be, and you begin to see op-eds like this one: "Why 2012 is shaping up as an 'Anybody But Obama' election."[219]

To quote Donald Trump, "Obama is the worst president this country has ever had." He's done more harm to Israel that anyone could have imagined in 2008, and he's doing his best to destroy the US too, BUT—and please pay attention—Obama can still win in 2012.

Don't think for one second that Obama can't win in 2012. He can win, and he will win if conservatives don't behave intelligently. A few conservative blunders and we guarantee FOUR MORE YEARS OF OBAMA.

The public faces of the Republican Party—people like Mitch McConnell and John Boehner—participated in the creation of the mess we're in. They've simply utilized one of the principle rules of politics: if you can't beat them, lead them. Deep down in their hearts, they aren't who they pretend to be, and they can blow it.

Let's face facts:

- Republicans control the House.

---

[219] http://washingtonexaminer.com/opinion/columnists/2011/07/why-2012-shaping-anybody-obama-election

- Democrats control the Senate.

- President Obama is in the Oval Office.

- It will take 2 more election cycles to rehabilitate the Senate.

- Our debt problem can explode at any time.

- It's time to elect people who care about solving our problems and healing our nation.

Whoever is elected President of the United States in 2012 will have to contend with the monumental problems that Obama's misguided policies have caused both at home and abroad. It's time to start thinking seriously about who that person should be. One thing is certain, though. It should not be Barack Obama.

Appendix

The Palestinian and Hamas Charters

The Palestinian National Charter

Al-Mithaq Al-Watanee Al-Philisteeni

July 17, 1968

Articles of the Charter:

Article 1:

Palestine is the homeland of the Arab Palestinian people; it is an indivisible part of the greater Arab homeland, and the Palestinian people are an integral part of the Arab nation.

Article 2:

Palestine, with the boundaries it had during the British Mandate, is an indivisible territorial unit.

Article 3:

The Palestinian Arab people possess the legal right to their homeland and to self-determination after the completion of the liberation of their country in accordance with their wishes and entirely of their own accord and will.

167

Article 4:

The Palestinian identity is a genuine, essential, and inherent characteristic; it is transmitted from fathers to children. The Zionist occupation and the dispersal of the Palestinian Arab people, through the disasters which befell them, do not make them lose their Palestinian identity and their membership in the Palestinian community, nor do they negate them.

Article 5:

The Palestinians are those Arab nationals who, until 1947, normally resided in Palestine regardless of whether they were evicted from it or stayed there. Anyone born, after that date, of a Palestinian father- whether in Palestine or outside it- is also a Palestinian.

Article 6:

The Jews who had normally resided in Palestine until the beginning of the Zionist invasion are considered Palestinians.

Article 7:

There is a Palestinian community and that it has material, spiritual, and historical connection with Palestine are indisputable facts. It is a national duty to bring up individual Palestinians in an Arab revolutionary manner. All means of information and education must be adopted in order to acquaint the Palestinian with his country in the most profound manner, both spiritual and material, that is possible. He must be prepared for the armed struggle and ready to sacrifice his wealth and his life in order to win back his homeland and bring about its liberation.

Article 8:

The phase in their history, through which the Palestinian people are now living, is that of national (watani) struggle for the liberation of Palestine. Thus the conflicts among the Palestinian national forces are secondary, and should be ended for the sake of the basic conflict that exists between the forces of Zionism and of colonialism on the one hand, and the Palestinian Arab people on the other. On this basis the Palestinian masses, regardless of whether they are residing in the national homeland or in Diaspora (mahajir) constitute- both their organizations and the individuals- one national front working for the retrieval of Palestine and its liberation through armed struggle.

Article 9:

Armed struggle is the only way to liberate Palestine. This is the overall strategy, not merely a tactical phase. The Palestinian Arab people assert their absolute determination and firm resolution to continue their armed struggle and to work for an armed popular revolution for the liberation of their country and their return to it. They also assert their right to normal life in Palestine and to exercise their right to self-determination and sovereignty over it.

Article 10:

Commando (Feday'ee) action constitutes the nucleus of the Palestinian popular liberation war. This requires its escalation, comprehensiveness, and the mobilization of all the Palestinian popular and educational efforts and their organization and involvement in the armed Palestinian revolution. It also requires the achieving of unity for the national (watani) struggle among the different groupings of the Palestinian people, and between the Palestinian people and the Arab masses, so as to secure the continuation of the revolution, its escalation, and victory.

Article 11:

Palestinians have three mottoes: national unity, national (al-qawmiyya) mobilization, and liberation.

Article 12:

The Palestinian Arab people believe in Arab unity. In order to contribute their share toward the attainment of that objective, however, they must, at the present stage of their struggle, safeguard their Palestinian identity and develop their consciousness of that identity, oppose any plan that may dissolve or impair it.

Article 13:

Arab unity and the liberation of Palestine are two complementary goals, the attainment of either of which facilitates the attainment of the other. Thus, Arab unity leads to the liberation of Palestine, the liberation of Palestine leads to Arab unity; and the work toward the realization of one objective proceeds side by side with work toward the realization of the other.

Article 14:

The destiny of the Arab Nation, and indeed Arab existence itself, depend upon the destiny of the Palestinian cause. From this interdependence springs the Arab nation's pursuit of, and striving for, the liberation of Palestine. The people of Palestine play the role of the vanguard in the realization of this sacred (qawmi) goal.

Article 15:

The liberation of Palestine, from an Arab viewpoint, is a national (qawmi) duty and it attempts to repel the Zionist and imperialist aggression against the Arab homeland, and aims at the elimination of Zionism in Palestine. Absolute responsibility for this falls upon the Arab nation- peoples and governments-with the Arab people of Palestine in the vanguard. Accordingly, the Arab nation must mobilize all its military, human, moral, and spiritual capabilities to participate actively with the Palestinian people in the liberation of Palestine. It must, particularly, in the phase of the armed Palestinian revolution, offer and furnish the Palestinian people with all possible help, and material and human support, and make available to them the means and opportunities that will enable them to continue to carry out their leading role in the armed revolution, until they liberate their homeland.

Article 16:

The liberation of Palestine, from a spiritual viewpoint, will provide the Holy Land with an atmosphere of safety and tranquillity, which in turn will safeguard the country's religious sanctuaries and guarantee freedom of worship and of visit to all, without discrimination of race, color, language, or religion. Accordingly, the Palestinian people look to all spiritual forces in the world for support.

Article 17:

The liberation of Palestine, from a human point of view, will restore to the Palestinian individual his dignity, pride, and freedom. Accordingly, the Palestinian Arab people look forward to the support of all those who believe in the dignity of man and his freedom in the world.

Article 18:

The liberation of Palestine, from an international point of view, is a defensive action necessitated by the demands of self-defense. Accordingly, the Palestinian people, desirous as they are of the friendship of all people, look to freedom-loving and peace-loving states for support in order to restore their legitimate rights in Palestine, to re-establish peace and security in the country, and to enable its people to exercise national sovereignty and freedom.

Article 19:

The partition of Palestine in 1947, and the establishment of the state of Israel are entirely illegal, regardless of the passage of time, because they were contrary to the will of the Palestinian people and its natural right in their homeland, and were inconsistent with the principles embodied in the Charter of the United Nations, particularly the right to self-determination.

Article 20:

The Balfour Declaration, the Palestine Mandate, and everything that has been based on them, are deemed null and void. Claims of historical or religious ties of Jews with Palestine are incompatible with the facts of history and the conception of what constitutes statehood. Judaism, being a religion, is not an independent nationality. Nor do Jews constitute a single nation with an identity of their own; they are citizens of the states to which they belong.

Article 21:

The Arab Palestinian people, expressing themselves by armed Palestinian revolution, reject all solutions which are substitutes for the total liberation of Palestine and reject all proposals aimed at the liquidation of the Palestinian cause, or at its internationalization.

Article 22:

Zionism is a political movement organically associated with international imperialism and antagonistic to all action for liberation and to progressive movements in the world. It is racist and fanatic in its nature, aggressive, expansionist and colonial in its aims, and fascist in its methods. Israel is the instrument of the Zionist movement, and the geographical base for world imperialism placed strategically in the midst of the Arab homeland to combat the hopes of the Arab nation for liberation, unity, and progress. Israel is a constant source of threat vis-à-vis peace in the Middle East and the whole world. Since liberation of Palestine will destroy the Zionist and imperialist presence and will contribute to the establishment of peace in the Middle East. That is why the Palestinian people look to the progressive and peaceful forces and urge them all, irrespective of their affiliations and beliefs, to offer the Palestinian people all aid and support in their just struggle for the liberation of their homeland.

Article 23:

The demand of security and peace, as well as the demand of right and justice, require all states to consider Zionism an illegitimate movement, to outlaw its existence, and to ban its operations, in order that friendly relations among peoples may be preserved, and the loyalty of citizens to their respective homelands safeguarded.

Article 24:

The Palestinian people believe in the principles of justice, freedom, sovereignty, self-determination, human dignity, and the right of peoples to exercise them.

Article 25:

For the realization of the goals of this Charter and its principles, the Palestine Liberation Organization will perform its role in the liberation of Palestine.

Article 26:

The Palestine Liberation Organization, the representative of the Palestinian revolutionary forces, is responsible for the Palestinian Arab peoples movement in its struggle- to retrieve its homeland, liberate and return to it and exercise the right to self-determination in it- in all military, political, and financial fields and also for whatever may be required by the Palestinian cause on the inter-Arab and international levels.

Article 27:

The Palestine Liberation Organization shall cooperate with all Arab states, each according to its potentialities; and will adopt a neutral policy among them in light of the requirements of the battle of liberation; and on this basis does not interfere in the internal affairs of any Arab state.

Article 28:

The Palestinian Arab people assert the genuineness and independence of their national revolution and reject all forms of intervention, trusteeship, and subordination.

Article 29:

The Palestinian people possess the fundamental and genuine legal right to liberate and retrieve their homeland. The Palestinian people determine their attitude toward all states and forces on the basis of the stands they adopt vis-à-vis the Palestinian revolution to fulfill the aims of the Palestinian people.

Article 30:

Fighters and carriers of arms in the war of liberation are the nucleus of the popular army which will be the protective force for the gains of the Palestinian Arab people.

Article 31:

This Organization shall have a flag, an oath of allegiance, and an anthem. All this shall be decided upon in accordance with a special law.

Article 32:

A law, known as the Basic Statute of the Palestine Liberation Organization, shall be annexed to this Covenant. It will lay down the manner in which the Organization, and its organs and institutions, shall be constituted; the respective competence of each; and the requirements of its obligation under the Charter.

Article 33:

This Charter shall not be amended save by [vote of] a majority of two-thirds of the total membership of the National Council of the Palestine Liberation Organization [taken] at a special session convened for that purpose.

****

The Covenant of the Islamic Resistance Movement (Hamas)

August 18, 1988

In The Name Of The Most Merciful Allah

"Ye are the best nation that hath been raised up unto mankind: ye command that which is just, and ye forbid that which is unjust, and ye believe in Allah. And if they who have received the scriptures had believed, it had surely been the better for them: there are believers among them, but the greater part of them are transgressors. They shall not hurt you, unless with a slight hurt; and if they fight against you, they shall turn their backs to you, and they shall not be helped. They are smitten with vileness wheresoever they are found; unless they obtain security by entering into a treaty with Allah, and a treaty with men; and they draw on themselves indignation from Allah, and they are afflicted with poverty. This they suffer, because they disbelieved the signs of Allah, and slew the prophets unjustly; this, because they were rebellious, and transgressed." (Al-Imran – verses 109-111).

Israel will exist and will continue to exist until Islam will obliterate it, just as it obliterated others before it" (The Martyr, Imam Hassan al-Banna, of blessed memory).

"The Islamic world is on fire. Each of us should pour some water, no matter how little, to extinguish whatever one can without waiting for the others." (Sheikh Amjad al-Zahawi, of blessed memory).

In The Name Of The Most Merciful Allah

Introduction:

Praise be unto Allah, to whom we resort for help, and whose forgiveness, guidance and support we seek; Allah bless the Prophet and grant him salvation, his companions and supporters, and to those who carried out his message and adopted his laws – everlasting prayers and salvation as long as the earth and heaven will last. Hereafter:

O People:

Out of the midst of troubles and the sea of suffering, out of the palpitations of faithful hearts and cleansed arms; out of the sense of duty, and in response to Allah's command, the call has gone out rallying people together and making them follow the ways of Allah, leading them to have determined will in order to fulfill their role in life, to overcome all obstacles, and surmount the difficulties on the way. Constant preparation has continued and so has the readiness to sacrifice life and all that is precious for the sake of Allah.

Thus it was that the nucleus (of the movement) was formed and started to pave its way through the tempestuous sea of hopes and expectations, of wishes and yearnings, of troubles and obstacles, of pain and challenges, both inside and outside.

When the idea was ripe, the seed grew and the plant struck root in the soil of reality, away from passing emotions, and hateful haste. The Islamic Resistance Movement emerged to carry out its role through striving for the sake of its Creator, its arms intertwined with those of all the fighters for the liberation of Palestine. The spirits of its fighters meet with the spirits of all the fighters who have sacrificed their lives on the soil of Palestine, ever since it was conquered by the companions of the Prophet, Allah bless him and grant him salvation, and until this day.

176

This Covenant of the Islamic Resistance Movement (HAMAS), clarifies its picture, reveals its identity, outlines its stand, explains its aims, speaks about its hopes, and calls for its support, adoption and joining its ranks. Our struggle against the Jews is very great and very serious. It needs all sincere efforts. It is a step that inevitably should be followed by other steps. The Movement is but one squadron that should be supported by more and more squadrons from this vast Arab and Islamic world, until the enemy is vanquished and Allah's victory is realised.

Thus we see them coming on the horizon "and you shall learn about it hereafter" "Allah hath written, Verily I will prevail, and my apostles: for Allah is strong and mighty." (The Dispute – verse 21).

"Say to them, This is my way: I invite you to Allah, by an evident demonstration; both I and he who followeth me; and, praise be unto Allah! I am not an idolator." (Joseph – verse 107).

Hamas (means) strength and bravery (according to) Al-Mua'jam al-Wasit: c1.

Definition of the Movement:

Ideological Starting-Points:

Article One:

The Islamic Resistance Movement: The Movement's programme is Islam. From it, it draws its ideas, ways of thinking and understanding of the universe, life and man. It resorts to it for judgement in all its conduct, and it is inspired by it for guidance of its steps.

The Islamic Resistance Movement's Relation With the Moslem Brotherhood Group:

Article Two:

The Islamic Resistance Movement is one of the wings of Moslem Brotherhood in Palestine. Moslem Brotherhood Movement is a universal organization which constitutes the largest Islamic movement in modern times. It is characterised by its deep understanding, accurate comprehension and its complete embrace of all Islamic concepts of all aspects of life, culture, creed, politics, economics, education, society, justice and judgement, the spreading of Islam, education, art, information, science of the occult and conversion to Islam.

Structure and Formation:

Article Three:

The basic structure of the Islamic Resistance Movement consists of Moslems who have given their allegiance to Allah whom they truly worship, – "I have created the jinn and humans only for the purpose of worshipping" – who know their duty towards themselves, their families and country. In all that, they fear Allah and raise the banner of Jihad in the face of the oppressors, so that they would rid the land and the people of their uncleanliness, vileness and evils.

"But we will oppose truth to vanity, and it shall confound the same; and behold, it shall vanish away." (Prophets – verse 18).

Article Four:

The Islamic Resistance Movement welcomes every Moslem who embraces its faith, ideology, follows its programme, keeps its secrets, and wants to belong to its ranks and carry out the duty. Allah will certainly reward such one.

Time and Place Extent of the Islamic Resistance Movement:

Article Five:

Time extent of the Islamic Resistance Movement: By adopting Islam as its way of life, the Movement goes back to the time of the birth of the Islamic message, of the righteous ancestor, for Allah is its target, the Prophet is its example and the Koran is its constitution. Its extent in place is anywhere that there are Moslems who embrace Islam as their way of life everywhere in the globe. This being so, it extends to the depth of the earth and reaches out to the heaven.

"Dost thou not see how Allah putteth forth a parable; representing a good word, as a good tree, whose root is firmly fixed in the earth, and whose branches reach unto heaven; which bringeth forth its fruit in all seasons, by the will of its Lord? Allah propoundeth parables unto men, that they may be instructed." (Abraham – verses 24-25).

Characteristics and Independence:

Article Six:

The Islamic Resistance Movement is a distinguished Palestinian movement, whose allegiance is to Allah, and whose way of life is Islam. It strives to raise the banner of Allah over every inch of Palestine, for under the wing of Islam followers of all religions can coexist in security and safety where their lives, possessions and rights are concerned. In the absence of Islam, strife will be rife, oppression spreads, evil prevails and schisms and wars will break out.

How excellent was the Moslem poet, Mohamed Ikbal, when he wrote:

"If faith is lost, there is no security and there is no life for him who does not adhere to religion. He who accepts life without religion, has taken annihilation as his companion for life."

The Universality of the Islamic Resistance Movement:

Article Seven:

As a result of the fact that those Moslems who adhere to the ways of the Islamic Resistance Movement spread all over the world, rally support for it and its stands, strive towards enhancing its struggle, the Movement is a universal one. It is well-equipped for that because of the clarity of its ideology, the nobility of its aim and the loftiness of its objectives.

On this basis, the Movement should be viewed and evaluated, and its role be recognised. He who denies its right, evades supporting it and turns a blind eye to facts, whether intentionally or unintentionally, would awaken to see that events have overtaken him and with no logic to justify his attitude. One should certainly learn from past examples.

The injustice of next-of-kin is harder to bear than the smite of the Indian sword.

"We have also sent down unto thee the book of the Koran with truth, confirming that scripture which was revealed before it; and preserving the same safe from corruption. Judge therefore between them according to that which Allah hath revealed; and follow not their desires, by swerving from the truth which hath come unto thee. Unto every of you have we given a law, and an open path; and if Allah had pleased, he had surely made you one people; but he hath thought it fit to give you different laws, that he might try you in that which he hath given you respectively. Therefore strive to excel each other in good works; unto Allah shall ye all return, and then will he declare unto you that concerning which ye have disagreed." (The Table, verse 48).

The Islamic Resistance Movement is one of the links in the chain of the struggle against the Zionist invaders. It goes back to 1939, to the emergence of the martyr Izz al-Din al Kissam and his brethren the fighters, members of Moslem Brotherhood. It goes on to reach out and become one with another chain that includes the struggle of the Palestinians and Moslem Brotherhood in the 1948 war and the Jihad operations of the Moslem Brotherhood in 1968 and after.

Moreover, if the links have been distant from each other and if obstacles, placed by those who are the lackeys of Zionism in the way of the fighters obstructed the continuation of the struggle, the Islamic Resistance Movement aspires to the realisation of Allah's promise, no matter how long that should take. The Prophet, Allah bless him and grant him salvation, has said:

"The Day of Judgement will not come about until Moslems fight the Jews (killing the Jews), when the Jew will hide behind stones and trees. The stones and trees will say O Moslems, O Abdulla, there is a Jew behind me, come and kill him. Only the Gharkad tree, (evidently a certain kind of tree) would not do that because it is one of the trees of the Jews." (related by al-Bukhari and Moslem).

The Slogan of the Islamic Resistance Movement:

Article Eight:

Allah is its target, the Prophet is its model, the Koran its constitution: Jihad is its path and death for the sake of Allah is the loftiest of its wishes.

Objectives

Incentives and Objectives:

Article Nine:

The Islamic Resistance Movement found itself at a time when Islam has disappeared from life. Thus rules shook, concepts were upset, values changed and evil people took control, oppression and darkness prevailed, cowards became like tigers: homelands were usurped, people were scattered and were caused to wander all over the world, the state of justice disappeared and the state of falsehood replaced it. Nothing remained in its right place. Thus, when Islam is absent from the arena, everything changes. From this state of affairs the incentives are drawn.

As for the objectives: They are the fighting against the false, defeating it and vanquishing it so that justice could prevail, homelands be retrieved and from its mosques would the voice of the mu'azen emerge declaring the establishment of the state of Islam, so that people and things would return each to their right places and Allah is our helper.

"...and if Allah had not prevented men, the one by the other, verily the earth had been corrupted: but Allah is beneficient towards his creatures." (The Cow – verse 251).

Article Ten:

As the Islamic Resistance Movement paves its way, it will back the oppressed and support the wronged with all its might. It will spare no effort to bring about justice and defeat injustice, in word and deed, in this place and everywhere it can reach and have influence therein.

Strategies and Methods:

Strategies of the Islamic Resistance Movement: Palestine Is Isalmic aqf:

Article Eleven:

The Islamic Resistance Movement believes that the land of Palestine is an Islamic Waqf consecrated for future Moslem generations until Judgement Day. It, or any part of it, should not be squandered: it, or any part of it, should not be given up. Neither a single Arab country nor all Arab countries, neither any king or president, nor all the kings and presidents, neither any organization nor all of them, be they Palestinian or Arab, possess the right to do that. Palestine is an Islamic Waqf land consecrated for Moslem generations until Judgement Day. This being so, who could claim to have the right to represent Moslem generations till Judgement Day?

This is the law governing the land of Palestine in the Islamic Sharia (law) and the same goes for any land the Moslems have conquered by force, because during the times of (Islamic) conquests, the Moslems consecrated these lands to Moslem generations till the Day of Judgement.

It happened like this: When the leaders of the Islamic armies conquered Syria and Iraq, they sent to the Caliph of the Moslems, Umar bin-el-Khatab, asking for his advice concerning the conquered land – whether they should divide it among the soldiers, or leave it for its owners, or what? After consultations and discussions between the Caliph of the Moslems, Omar bin-el-Khatab and companions of the Prophet, Allah bless him and grant him salvation, it was decided that the land should be left with its owners who could benefit by its fruit. As for the real ownership of the land and the land itself, it should be consecrated for Moslem generations till Judgement Day. Those who are on the land, are there only to benefit from its fruit. This Waqf remains as long as earth and heaven remain. Any procedure in contradiction to Islamic Sharia, where Palestine is concerned, is null and void.

"Verily, this is a certain truth. Wherefore praise the name of thy Lord, the great Allah." (The Inevitable – verse 95).

Homeland and Nationalism from the Point of View of the Islamic Resistance Movement in Palestine:

Article Twelve:

Nationalism, from the point of view of the Islamic Resistance Movement, is part of the religious creed. Nothing in nationalism is more significant or deeper than in the case when an enemy should tread Moslem land. Resisting and quelling the enemy become the individual duty of every Moslem, male or female. A woman can go out to fight the enemy without her husband's permission, and so does the slave: without his master's permission.

Nothing of the sort is to be found in any other regime. This is an undisputed fact. If other nationalist movements are connected with materialistic, human or regional causes, nationalism of the Islamic Resistance Movement has all these elements as well as the more important elements that give it soul and life. It is connected to the source of spirit and the granter of life, hoisting in the sky of the homeland the heavenly banner that joins earth and heaven with a strong bond.

If Moses comes and throws his staff, both witch and magic are annulled.

183

"Now is the right direction manifestly distinguished from deceit: whoever therefore shall deny Tagut, and believe in Allah, he shall surely take hold with a strong handle, which shall not be broken; Allah is he who heareth and seeth." (The Cow – Verse 256).

Peaceful Solutions, Initiatives and International Conferences:

Article Thirteen:

Initiatives, and so-called peaceful solutions and international conferences, are in contradiction to the principles of the Islamic Resistance Movement. Abusing any part of Palestine is abuse directed against part of religion. Nationalism of the Islamic Resistance Movement is part of its religion. Its members have been fed on that. For the sake of hoisting the banner of Allah over their homeland they fight. "Allah will be prominent, but most people do not know."

Now and then the call goes out for the convening of an international conference to look for ways of solving the (Palestinian) question. Some accept, others reject the idea, for this or other reason, with one stipulation or more for consent to convening the conference and participating in it. Knowing the parties constituting the conference, their past and present attitudes towards Moslem problems, the Islamic Resistance Movement does not consider these conferences capable of realising the demands, restoring the rights or doing justice to the oppressed. These conferences are only ways of setting the infidels in the land of the Moslems as arbitraters. When did the infidels do justice to the believers?

"But the Jews will not be pleased with thee, neither the Christians, until thou follow their religion; say, The direction of Allah is the true direction. And verily if thou follow their desires, after the knowledge which hath been given thee, thou shalt find no patron or protector against Allah." (The Cow – verse 120).

There is no solution for the Palestinian question except through Jihad. Initiatives, proposals and international conferences are all a waste of time and vain endeavors. The Palestinian people know better than to consent to having their future, rights and fate toyed with. As in said in the honourable Hadith:

"The people of Syria are Allah's lash in His land. He wreaks His vengeance through them against whomsoever He wishes among His slaves It is unthinkable that those who are double-faced among them should prosper over the faithful. They will certainly die out of grief and desperation."

The Three Circles:

Article Fourteen:

The question of the liberation of Palestine is bound to three circles: the Palestinian circle, the Arab circle and the Islamic circle. Each of these circles has its role in the struggle against Zionism. Each has its duties, and it is a horrible mistake and a sign of deep ignorance to overlook any of these circles. Palestine is an Islamic land which has the first of the two kiblahs (direction to which Moslems turn in praying), the third of the holy (Islamic) sanctuaries, and the point of departure for Mohamed's midnight journey to the seven heavens (i.e. Jerusalem).

"Praise be unto him who transported his servant by night, from the sacred temple of Mecca to the farther temple of Jerusalem, the circuit of which we have blessed, that we might show him some of our signs; for Allah is he who heareth, and seeth." (The Night-Journey – verse 1).

Since this is the case, liberation of Palestine is then an individual duty for very Moslem wherever he may be. On this basis, the problem should be viewed. This should be realised by every Moslem.

The day the problem is dealt with on this basis, when the three circles mobilize their capabilities, the present state of affairs will change and the day of liberation will come nearer.

"Verily ye are stronger than they, by reason of the terror cast into their breasts from Allah. This, because they are not people of prudence." (The Emigration – verse 13).

The Jihad for the Liberation of Palestine is an Individual Duty:

Article Fifteen:

The day that enemies usurp part of Moslem land, Jihad becomes the individual duty of every Moslem. In face of the Jews' usurpation of Palestine, it is compulsory that the banner of Jihad be raised. To do this requires the diffusion of Islamic consciousness among the masses, both on the regional, Arab and Islamic levels. It is necessary to instill the spirit of Jihad in the heart of the nation so that they would confront the enemies and join the ranks of the fighters.

It is necessary that scientists, educators and teachers, information and media people, as well as the educated masses, especially the youth and sheikhs of the Islamic movements, should take part in the operation of awakening (the masses). It is important that basic changes be made in the school curriculum, to cleanse it of the traces of ideological invasion that affected it as a result of the orientalists and missionaries who infiltrated the region following the defeat of the Crusaders at the hands of Salah el-Din (Saladin). The Crusaders realised that it was impossible to defeat the Moslems without first having ideological invasion pave the way by upsetting their thoughts, disfiguring their heritage and violating their ideals. Only then could they invade with soldiers. This, in its turn, paved the way for the imperialistic invasion that made Allenby declare on entering Jerusalem: "Only now have the Crusades ended." General Guru stood at Salah el-Din's grave and said: "We have returned, O Salah el-Din." Imperialism has helped towards the strengthening of ideological invasion, deepening, and still does, its roots. All this has paved the way towards the loss of Palestine.

It is necessary to instill in the minds of the Moslem generations that the Palestinian problem is a religious problem, and should be dealt with on this basis. Palestine contains Islamic holy sites. In it there is al- Aqsa Mosque which is bound to the great Mosque in Mecca in an inseparable bond as long as heaven and earth speak of Isra` (Mohammed's midnight journey to the seven heavens) and Mi'raj (Mohammed's ascension to the seven heavens from Jerusalem).

"The bond of one day for the sake of Allah is better than the world and whatever there is on it. The place of one's whip in Paradise is far better than the world and whatever there is on it. A worshipper's going and coming in the service of Allah is better than the world and whatever there is on it." (As related by al-Bukhari, Moslem, al-Tarmdhi and Ibn Maja).

"I swear by the holder of Mohammed's soul that I would like to invade and be killed for the sake of Allah, then invade and be killed, and then invade again and be killed." (As related by al-Bukhari and Moslem).

The Education of the Generations:

Article Sixteen:

It is necessary to follow Islamic orientation in educating the Islamic generations in our region by teaching the religious duties, comprehensive study of the Koran, the study of the Prophet's Sunna (his sayings and doings), and learning about Islamic history and heritage from their authentic sources. This should be done by specialised and learned people, using a curriculum that would healthily form the thoughts and faith of the Moslem student. Side by side with this, a comprehensive study of the enemy, his human and financial capabilities, learning about his points of weakness and strength, and getting to know the forces supporting and helping him, should also be included. Also, it is important to be acquainted with the current events, to follow what is new and to study the analysis and commentaries made of these events. Planning for the present and future, studying every trend appearing, is a must so that the fighting Moslem would live knowing his aim, objective and his way in the midst of what is going on around him.

"O my son, verily every matter, whether good or bad, though it be the weight of a grain of mustard-seed, and be hidden in a rock, or in the heavens, or in the earth, Allah will bring the same to light; for Allah is clear-sighted and knowing. O my son, be constant at prayer, and command that which is just, and forbid that which is evil: and be patient under the afflictions which shall befall thee; for this is a duty absolutely incumbent on all men. Distort not thy face out of contempt to men, neither walk in the earth with insolence; for Allah loveth no arrogant, vain-glorious person." (Lokman – verses 16-18).

187

The Role of the Moslem Woman:

Article Seventeen:

The Moslem woman has a role no less important than that of the moslem man in the battle of liberation. She is the maker of men. Her role in guiding and educating the new generations is great. The enemies have realised the importance of her role. They consider that if they are able to direct and bring her up they way they wish, far from Islam, they would have won the battle. That is why you find them giving these attempts constant attention through information campaigns, films, and the school curriculum, using for that purpose their lackeys who are infiltrated through Zionist organizations under various names and shapes, such as Freemasons, Rotary Clubs, espionage groups and others, which are all nothing more than cells of subversion and saboteurs. These organizations have ample resources that enable them to play their role in societies for the purpose of achieving the Zionist targets and to deepen the concepts that would serve the enemy. These organizations operate in the absence of Islam and its estrangement among its people. The Islamic peoples should perform their role in confronting the conspiracies of these saboteurs. The day Islam is in control of guiding the affairs of life, these organizations, hostile to humanity and Islam, will be obliterated.

Article Eighteen:

Woman in the home of the fighting family, whether she is a mother or a sister, plays the most important role in looking after the family, rearing the children and embuing them with moral values and thoughts derived from Islam. She has to teach them to perform the religious duties in preparation for the role of fighting awaiting them. That is why it is necessary to pay great attention to schools and the curriculum followed in educating Moslem girls, so that they would grow up to be good mothers, aware of their role in the battle of liberation.

She has to be of sufficient knowledge and understanding where the performance of housekeeping matters are concerned, because economy and avoidance of waste of the family budget, is one of the requirements for the ability to continue moving forward in the difficult conditions surrounding us. She should put before her eyes the fact that the money available to her is just like blood which should never flow except through the veins so that both children and grown-ups could continue to live.

"Verily, the Moslems of either sex, and the true believers of either sex, and the devout men, and the devout women, and the men of veracity, and the women of veracity, and the patient men, and the patient women, and the humble men, and the humble women, and the alms-givers of either sex who remember Allah frequently; for them hath Allah prepared forgiveness and a great reward." (The Confederates – verse 25).

The Role of Islamic Art in the Battle of Liberation:

Article Nineteen:

Art has regulations and measures by which it can be determined whether it is Islamic or pre-Islamic (Jahili) art. The issues of Islamic liberation are in need of Islamic art that would take the spirit high, without raising one side of human nature above the other, but rather raise all of them harmoniously an in equilibrium.

Man is a unique and wonderful creature, made out of a handful of clay and a breath from Allah. Islamic art addresses man on this basis, while pre-Islamic art addresses the body giving preference to the clay component in it.

The book, the article, the bulletin, the sermon, the thesis, the popular poem, the poetic ode, the song, the play and others, contain the characteristics of Islamic art, then these are among the requirements of ideological mobilization, renewed food for the journey and recreation for the soul. The road is long and suffering is plenty. The soul will be bored, but Islamic art renews the energies, resurrects the movement, arousing in them lofty meanings and proper conduct. "Nothing can improve the self if it is in retreat except shifting from one mood to another."

All this is utterly serious and no jest, for those who are fighters do not jest.

Social Mutual Responsibility:

Article Twenty:

Moslem society is a mutually responsible society. The Prophet, prayers and greetings be unto him, said: "Blessed are the generous, whether they were in town or on a journey, who have collected all that they had and shared it equally among themselves."

The Islamic spirit is what should prevail in every Moslem society. The society that confronts a vicious enemy which acts in a way similar to Nazism, making no differentiation between man and woman, between children and old people – such a society is entitled to this Islamic spirit. Our enemy relies on the methods of collective punishment. He has deprived people of their homeland and properties, pursued them in their places of exile and gathering, breaking bones, shooting at women, children and old people, with or without a reason. The enemy has opened detention camps where thousands and thousands of people are thrown and kept under sub-human conditions. Added to this, are the demolition of houses, rendering children orphans, meting cruel sentences against thousands of young people, and causing them to spend the best years of their lives in the dungeons of prisons.

In their Nazi treatment, the Jews made no exception for women or children. Their policy of striking fear in the heart is meant for all. They attack people where their breadwinning is concerned, extorting their money and threatening their honour. They deal with people as if they were the worst war criminals. Deportation from the homeland is a kind of murder.

To counter these deeds, it is necessary that social mutual responsibility should prevail among the people. The enemy should be faced by the people as a single body which if one member of it should complain, the rest of the body would respond by feeling the same pains.

Article Twenty-One:

Mutual social responsibility means extending assistance, financial or moral, to all those who are in need and joining in the execution of some of the work. Members of the Islamic Resistance Movement should consider the interests of the masses as their own

190

personal interests. They must spare no effort in achieving and preserving them. They must prevent any foul play with the future of the upcoming generations and anything that could cause loss to society. The masses are part of them and they are part of the masses. Their strength is theirs, and their future is theirs. Members of the Islamic Resistance Movement should share the people's joy and grief, adopt the demands of the public and whatever means by which they could be realised. The day that such a spirit prevails, brotherliness would deepen, cooperation, sympathy and unity will be enhanced and the ranks will be solidified to confront the enemies.

Supportive Forces Behind the Enemy:

Article Twenty-Two:

For a long time, the enemies have been planning, skillfully and with precision, for the achievement of what they have attained. They took into consideration the causes affecting the current of events. They strived to amass great and substantive material wealth which they devoted to the realisation of their dream. With their money, they took control of the world media, news agencies, the press, publishing houses, broadcasting stations, and others. With their money they stirred revolutions in various parts of the world with the purpose of achieving their interests and reaping the fruit therein. They were behind the French Revolution, the Communist revolution and most of the revolutions we heard and hear about, here and there. With their money they formed secret societies, such as Freemasons, Rotary Clubs, the Lions and others in different parts of the world for the purpose of sabotaging societies and achieving Zionist interests. With their money they were able to control imperialistic countries and instigate them to colonize many countries in order to enable them to exploit their resources and spread corruption there.

You may speak as much as you want about regional and world wars. They were behind World War I, when they were able to destroy the Islamic Caliphate, making financial gains and controlling resources. They obtained the Balfour Declaration, formed the League of Nations through which they could rule the world. They were behind World War II, through which they made huge financial gains by trading in armaments, and paved the way for the establishment of their state. It was they who instigated the replacement of the League of Nations with the United Nations and the Security Council to enable them to rule the world through them. There is no war going on anywhere, without having their finger in it.

"So often as they shall kindle a fire for war, Allah shall extinguish it; and they shall set their minds to act corruptly in the earth, but Allah loveth not the corrupt doers." (The Table – verse 64).

The imperialistic forces in the Capitalist West and Communist East, support the enemy with all their might, in money and in men. These forces take turns in doing that. The day Islam appears, the forces of infidelity would unite to challenge it, for the infidels are of one nation.

"O true believers, contract not an intimate friendship with any besides yourselves: they will not fail to corrupt you. They wish for that which may cause you to perish: their hatred hath already appeared from out of their mouths; but what their breasts conceal is yet more inveterate. We have already shown you signs of their ill will towards you, if ye understand." (The Family of Imran – verse 118).

It is not in vain that the verse is ended with Allah's words "if ye understand."

Our Attitudes Towards:

A. Islamic Movements:

Article Twenty-Three:

The Islamic Resistance Movement views other Islamic movements with respect and appreciation. If it were at variance with them on one point or opinion, it is in agreement with them on other points and understandings. It considers these movements, if they reveal good intentions and dedication to Allah, that they fall into the category of those who are trying hard since they act within the Islamic circle. Each active person has his share.

The Islamic Resistance Movement considers all these movements as a fund for itself. It prays to Allah for guidance and directions for all and it spares no effort to keep the banner of unity raised, ever striving for its realisation in accordance with the Koran and the Prophet's directives.

"And cleave all of you unto the covenant of Allah, and depart not from it, and remember the favour of Allah towards you: since ye were enemies, and he reconciled your hearts, and ye became companions and brethren by his favour: and ye were on the brink of a pit of fire, and he delivered you thence. Allah declareth unto you his signs, that ye may be directed." (The Family of Imran – Verse 102).

Article Twenty-Four:

The Islamic Resistance Movement does not allow slandering or speaking ill of individuals or groups, for the believer does not indulge in such malpractices. It is necessary to differentiate between this behaviour and the stands taken by certain individuals and groups. Whenever those stands are erroneous, the Islamic Resistance Movement preserves the right to expound the error and to warn against it. It will strive to show the right path and to judge the case in question with objectivity. Wise conduct is indeed the target of the believer who follows it wherever he discerns it.

"Allah loveth not the speaking ill of anyone in public, unless he who is injured call for assistance; and Allah heareth and knoweth: whether ye publish a good action, or conceal it, or forgive evil, verily Allah is gracious and powerful." (Women – verses 147-148).

B. Nationalist Movements in the Palestinian Arena:

Article Twenty-Five:

The Islamic Resistance Movement respects these movements and appreciates their circumstances and the conditions surrounding and affecting them. It encourages them as long as they do not give their allegiance to the Communist East or the Crusading West. It confirms to all those who are integrated in it, or sympathetic towards it, that the Islamic Resistance Movement is a fighting movement that has a moral and enlightened look of life and the way it should cooperate with the other (movements). It detests opportunism and desires only the good of people, individuals and groups alike. It does not seek material gains, personal fame, nor does it look for a reward from others. It works with its own resources and whatever is at its disposal "and prepare for them whatever force you can", for the fulfilment of the duty, and the earning of Allah's favour. It has no other desire than that.

The Movement assures all the nationalist trends operating in the Palestinian arena for the liberation of Palestine, that it is there for their support and assistance. It will never be more than that, both in words and deeds, now and in the future. It is there to bring together and not to divide, to preserve and not to squander, to unify and not to throw asunder. It evaluates every good word, sincere effort and good offices. It closes the door in the face of side disagreements and does not lend an ear to rumours and slanders, while at the same time fully realising the right for self-defence.

Anything contrary or contradictory to these trends, is a lie disseminated by enemies or their lackeys for the purpose of sowing confusion, disrupting the ranks and occupy them with side issues.

"O true believers, if a wicked man come unto you with a tale, inquire strictly into the truth thereof; lest ye hurt people through ignorance, and afterwards repent of what ye have done." (The Inner Apartments – verse 6).

Article Twenty-Six:

In viewing the Palestinian nationalist movements that give allegiance neither to the East nor the West, in this positive way, the Islamic Resistance Movement does not refrain from discussing new situations on the regional or international levels where the Palestinian question is concerned. It does that in such an objective manner revealing the extent of how much it is in harmony or contradiction with the national interests in the light of the Islamic point of view.

C. The Palestinian Liberation Organization:

Article Twenty-Seven:

The Palestinian Liberation Organization is the closest to the heart of the Islamic Resistance Movement. It contains the father and the brother, the next of kin and the friend. The Moslem does not estrange himself from his father, brother, next of kin or friend. Our homeland is one, our situation is one, our fate is one and the enemy is a joint enemy to all of us.

Because of the situations surrounding the formation of the Organization, of the ideological confusion prevailing in the Arab world as a result of the ideological invasion under whose influence the Arab world has fallen since the defeat of the Crusaders and which was, and still is, intensified through orientalists, missionaries and imperialists, the Organization adopted the idea of the secular state. And that it how we view it.

Secularism completely contradicts religious ideology. Attitudes, conduct and decisions stem from ideologies.

That is why, with all our appreciation for The Palestinian Liberation Organization – and what it can develop into – and without belittling its role in the Arab-Israeli conflict, we are unable to exchange the present or future Islamic Palestine with the secular idea. The Islamic nature of Palestine is part of our religion and whoever takes his religion lightly is a loser.

"Who will be adverse to the religion of Abraham, but he whose mind is infatuated? (The Cow – verse 130).

The day The Palestinian Liberation Organization adopts Islam as its way of life, we will become its soldiers, and fuel for its fire that will burn the enemies.

Until such a day, and we pray to Allah that it will be soon, the Islamic Resistance Movement's stand towards the PLO is that of the son towards his father, the brother towards his brother, and the relative to relative, suffers his pain and supports him in confronting the enemies, wishing him to be wise and well-guided.

"Stand by your brother, for he who is brotherless is like the fighter who goes to battle without arms. One's cousin is the wing one flies with – could the bird fly without wings?"

D. Arab and Islamic Countries:

Article Twenty-Eight:

The Zionist invasion is a vicious invasion. It does not refrain from resorting to all methods, using all evil and contemptible ways to achieve its end. It relies greatly in its infiltration and espionage operations on the secret organizations it gave rise to, such as the Freemasons, The Rotary and Lions clubs, and other sabotage groups. All these organizations, whether secret or open, work in the interest of Zionism and according to its instructions. They aim at undermining societies, destroying values, corrupting consciences, deteriorating character and annihilating Islam. It is behind the drug trade and alcoholism in all its kinds so as to facilitate its control and expansion.

Arab countries surrounding Israel are asked to open their borders before the fighters from among the Arab and Islamic nations so that they could consolidate their efforts with those of their Moslem brethren in Palestine.

As for the other Arab and Islamic countries, they are asked to facilitate the movement of the fighters from and to it, and this is the least thing they could do.

We should not forget to remind every Moslem that when the Jews conquered the Holy City in 1967, they stood on the threshold of the Aqsa Mosque and proclaimed that "Mohammed is dead, and his descendants are all women."

Israel, Judaism and Jews challenge Islam and the Moslem people. "May the cowards never sleep."

E. Nationalist and Religious Groupings, Institutions, Intellectuals, The Arab and Islamic World:

The Islamic Resistance Movement hopes that all these groupings will side with it in all spheres, would support it, adopt its stand and solidify its activities and moves, work towards rallying support for it so that the Islamic people will be a base and a stay for it, supplying it with strategic depth an all human material and informative spheres, in time and in place. This should be done through the convening of solidarity conferences, the issuing of explanatory bulletins, favourable articles and booklets, enlightening the masses regarding the Palestinian issue, clarifying what confronts it and the conspiracies woven around it. They should mobilize the Islamic nations, ideologically, educationally and culturally, so that these peoples would be equipped to perform their role in the decisive battle of liberation, just as they did when they vanquished the Crusaders and the Tatars and saved human civilization. Indeed, that is not difficult for Allah.

"Allah hath written, Verily I will prevail, and my apostles: for Allah is strong and mighty." (The Dispute – verse 21).

Article Thirty:

Writers, intellectuals, media people, orators, educaters and teachers, and all the various sectors in the Arab and Islamic world – all of them are called upon to perform their role, and to fulfill their duty, because of the ferocity of the Zionist offensive and the Zionist influence in many countries exercised through financial and media control, as well as the consequences that all this lead to in the greater part of the world.

Jihad is not confined to the carrying of arms and the confrontation of the enemy. The effective word, the good article, the useful book, support and solidarity – together with the presence of sincere purpose for the hoisting of Allah's banner higher and higher – all these are elements of the Jihad for Allah's sake.

"Whosoever mobilises a fighter for the sake of Allah is himself a fighter. Whosoever supports the relatives of a fighter, he himself is a fighter." (related by al-Bukhari, Moslem, Abu-Dawood and al-Tarmadhi).

F. Followers of Other Religions: The Islamic Resistance Movement Is A Humanistic Movement:

Article Thirty-One:

The Islamic Resistance Movement is a humanistic movement. It takes care of human rights and is guided by Islamic tolerance when dealing with the followers of other religions. It does not antagonize anyone of them except if it is antagonized by it or stands in its way to hamper its moves and waste its efforts.

Under the wing of Islam, it is possible for the followers of the three religions – Islam, Christianity and Judaism – to coexist in peace and quiet with each other. Peace and quiet would not be possible except under the wing of Islam. Past and present history are the best witness to that.

It is the duty of the followers of other religions to stop disputing the sovereignty of Islam in this region, because the day these followers should take over there will be nothing but carnage, displacement and terror. Everyone of them is at variance with his fellow-religionists, not to speak about followers of other religionists. Past and present history are full of examples to prove this fact.

"They will not fight against you in a body, except in fenced towns, or from behind walls. Their strength in war among themselves is great: thou thinkest them to be united; but their hearts are divided. This, because they are people who do not understand." (The Emigration – verse 14).

Islam confers upon everyone his legitimate rights. Islam prevents the incursion on other people's rights. The Zionist Nazi activities against our people will not last for long. "For the state of injustice lasts but one day, while the state of justice lasts till Doomsday."

"As to those who have not borne arms against you on account of religion, nor turned you out of your dwellings, Allah forbiddeth you not to deal kindly with them, and to behave justly towards them; for Allah loveth those who act justly." (The Tried – verse 8).

The Attempt to Isolate the Palestinian People:

Article Thirty-Two:

World Zionism, together with imperialistic powers, try through a studied plan and an intelligent strategy to remove one Arab state after another from the circle of struggle against Zionism, in order to have it finally face the Palestinian people only. Egypt was, to a great extent, removed from the circle of the struggle, through the treacherous Camp David Agreement. They are trying to draw other Arab countries into similar agreements and to bring them outside the circle of struggle.

The Islamic Resistance Movement calls on Arab and Islamic nations to take up the line of serious and persevering action to prevent the success of this horrendous plan, to warn the people of the danger eminating from leaving the circle of struggle against Zionism. Today it is Palestine, tomorrow it will be one country or another. The Zionist plan is limitless. After Palestine, the Zionists aspire to expand from the Nile to the Euphrates. When they will have digested the region they overtook, they will aspire to further expansion, and so on. Their plan is embodied in the "Protocols of the Elders of Zion", and their present conduct is the best proof of what we are saying.

Leaving the circle of struggle with Zionism is high treason, and cursed be he who does that. "for whoso shall turn his back unto them on that day, unless he turneth aside to fight, or retreateth to another party of the faithful, shall draw on himself the indignation of Allah, and his abode shall be hell; an ill journey shall it be thither." (The Spoils – verse 16). There is no way out except by concentrating all powers and energies to face this Nazi, vicious Tatar invasion. The alternative is loss of one's country, the dispersion of citizens, the spread of vice on earth and the destruction of religious values. Let every person know that he is responsible before Allah, for "the doer of the slightest good deed is rewarded in like, and the does of the slightest evil deed is also rewarded in like."

The Islamic Resistance Movement consider itself to be the spearhead of the circle of struggle with world Zionism and a step on the road. The Movement adds its efforts to the efforts of all those who are active in the Palestinian arena. Arab and Islamic Peoples should augment by further steps on their part; Islamic groupings all over the Arab world should also do the same, since all of these are the best-equipped for the future role in the fight with the warmongering Jews.

"..and we have put enmity and hatred between them, until the day of resurrection. So often as they shall kindle a fire of war, Allah shall extinguish it; and they shall set their minds to act corruptly in the earth, but Allah loveth not the corrupt doers." (The Table – verse 64).

Article Thirty-Three:

The Islamic Resistance Movement, being based on the common coordinated and interdependent conceptions of the laws of the universe, and flowing in the stream of destiny in confronting and fighting the enemies in defence of the Moslems and Islamic civilization and sacred sites, the first among which is the Aqsa Mosque, urges the Arab and Islamic peoples, their governments, popular and official groupings, to fear Allah where their view of the Islamic Resistance Movement and their dealings with it are concerned. They should back and support it, as Allah wants them to, extending to it more and more funds till Allah's purpose is achieved when ranks will close up, fighters join other fighters and masses everywhere in the Islamic world will come forward in response to the call of duty while loudly proclaiming: Hail to Jihad. Their cry will reach the heavens and will go on being resounded until liberation is achieved, the invaders vanquished and Allah's victory comes about.

"And Allah will certainly assist him who shall be on his side: for Allah is strong and mighty." (The Pilgrimage – verse 40).

The Testimony of History

Across History in Confronting the Invaders:

Article Thirty-Four:

Palestine is the navel of the globe and the crossroad of the continents. Since the dawn of history, it has been the target of expansionists. The Prophet, Allah bless him and grant him salvation, had himself pointed to this fact in the noble Hadith in which he called on his honourable companion, Ma'adh ben-Jabal, saying: O Ma'ath, Allah throw open before you, when I am gone, Syria, from Al-Arish to the Euphrates. Its men, women and slaves will stay firmly there till the Day of Judgement. Whoever of you should choose one of the Syrian shores, or the Holy Land, he will be in constant struggle till the Day of Judgement."

Expansionists have more than once put their eye on Palestine which they attacked with their armies to fulfill their designs on it. Thus it was that the Crusaders came with their armies, bringing with them their creed and carrying their Cross. They were able to defeat the Moslems for a while, but the Moslems were able to retrieve the land only when they stood under the wing of their religious banner, united their word, hallowed the name of Allah and surged out fighting under the leadership of Salah ed-Din al-Ayyubi. They fought for almost twenty years and at the end the Crusaders were defeated and Palestine was liberated.

"Say unto those who believe not, Ye shall be overcome, and thrown together into hell; an unhappy couch it shall be." (The Family of Imran – verse 12).

This is the only way to liberate Palestine. There is no doubt about the testimony of history. It is one of the laws of the universe and one of the rules of existence. Nothing can overcome iron except iron. Their false futile creed can only be defeated by the righteous Islamic creed. A creed could not be fought except by a creed, and in the last analysis, victory is for the just, for justice is certainly victorious.

"Our word hath formerly been given unto our servants the apostles; that they should certainly be assisted against the infidels, and that our armies should surely be the conquerors." (Those Who Rank Themselves – verses 171-172).

Article Thirty-Five:

The Islamic Resistance Movement views seriously the defeat of the Crusaders at the hands of Salah ed-Din al-Ayyubi and the rescuing of Palestine from their hands, as well as the defeat of the Tatars at Ein Galot, breaking their power at the hands of Qataz and Al-Dhaher Bivers and saving the Arab world from the Tatar onslaught which aimed at the destruction of every meaning of human civilization. The Movement draws lessons and examples from all this. The present Zionist onslaught has also been preceded by Crusading raids from the West and other Tatar raids from the East. Just as the Moslems faced those raids and planned fighting and defeating them, they should be able to confront the Zionist invasion and defeat it. This is indeed no problem for the Almighty Allah, provided that the intentions are pure, the determination is true and that Moslems have benefited from past experiences, rid themselves of the effects of ideological invasion and followed the customs of their ancestors.

The Islamic Resistance Movement is Composed of Soldiers:

Article Thirty-Six:

While paving its way, the Islamic Resistance Movement, emphasizes time and again to all the sons of our people, to the Arab and Islamic nations, that it does not seek personal fame, material gain, or social prominence. It does not aim to compete against any one from among our people, or take his place. Nothing of the sort at all. It will not act against any of the sons of Moslems or those who are peaceful towards it from among non-Moslems, be they here or anywhere else. It will only serve as a support for all groupings and organizations operating against the Zionist enemy and its lackeys.

The Islamic Resistance Movement adopts Islam as its way of life. Islam is its creed and religion. Whoever takes Islam as his way of life, be it an organization, a grouping, a country or any other body, the Islamic Resistance Movement considers itself as their soldiers and nothing more.

We ask Allah to show us the right course, to make us an example to others and to judge between us and our people with truth. "O Lord, do thou judge between us and our nation with truth; for thou art the best judge." (Al Araf – Verse 89).

The last of our prayers will be praise to Allah, the Master of the Universe.

www.ingramcontent.com/pod-product-compliance
Lightning Source LLC
Chambersburg PA
CBHW060252290526
45789CB00001B/294